Alfred Parsons

Notes in Japan

Alfred Parsons

Notes in Japan

ISBN/EAN: 9783337171032

Printed in Europe, USA, Canada, Australia, Japan

Cover: Foto ©Andreas Hilbeck / pixelio.de

More available books at **www.hansebooks.com**

NOTES IN JAPAN

BY

ALFRED PARSONS

WITH ILLUSTRATIONS BY THE AUTHOR

NEW YORK
HARPER & BROTHERS PUBLISHERS
1896

粟百合さん

CONTENTS

	PAGE
THE JAPANESE SPRING	3
EARLY SUMMER IN JAPAN	45
THE TIME OF THE LOTUS	81
FUJISAN	119
AUTUMN IN JAPAN	153
SOME WANDERINGS IN JAPAN	189

ILLUSTRATIONS

	PAGE
IN KASUGA PARK, NARA—AN OLD CRYPTOMERIA	*Frontispiece*
DEDICATION	vii
CHERRY-BLOSSOM BADGE, YOSHINO	2
IN THE INLAND SEA	4
HILLS NEAR KŌBE, FROM SUWA-YAMA	5
EARLY PLUM BLOSSOMS, OKAMOTO, NEAR KŌBE	7
THE TORII OF KASUGA TEMPLE, NARA	11
OLD WISTARIA IN KASUGA PARK, NARA	13
THE PAGODA OF KOBŪKUJI, NARA	14
CHERRY-TREE AND LANTERNS, NI-GWATSU-DŌ, NARA	15
THE WELL OF SANKATCHU, NARA	17
CHERRY BLOSSOMS IN THE RAIN, NARA	19
SARA-HIKI-SAKA, NEAR YOSHINO—LATER CHERRIES	21
CHERRY AND LATE PLUM, TEMA-CHO, NEAR NARA	23
A BUDDHIST TEMPLE AT YOSHINO—DOUBLE-FLOWERED CHERRY AND MAGNOLIA	27
CROSSING THE FERRY AT MUDA, ON THE YOSHINO-GAWA	30
MI KOMORI JINJA, A SHINTO TEMPLE NEAR YOSHINO	31
THE STREET, HASE	34
ANDROMEDA BUSHES IN KASUGA PARK, NARA	35
WHITE WISTARIA, HASE-DERA	37
A TALL WISTARIA, KASUGA PARK, NARA	39
NOTES AT MUDA	41
BADGE OF THE KIKU-SUI-YA	42

	PAGE
IRIS JAPONICA	44
CARRYING HOME TEA LEAVES, NEAR UJI	46
A PLANTATION COVERED WITH MATTING NEAR UJI	47
POND IN THE GARDEN OF RAKU-RAKU-TEI, HIKONE	49
THE CASTLE AT HIKONE	51
THE CASTLE AT NAGOYA, FIELD OF IRIS IN THE FOREGROUND	52
AN OLD CASTLE MOAT, AKASHI, NEAR KŌBE	53
FIELDS NEAR LAKE BIWA	55
O KAZU SAN	57
PREPARING THE RICE-FIELDS	59
MY ROOMS AT TENNENJI	60
BUDDHA AND HIS DISCIPLES, TENNENJI	61
HIKONE AND LAKE BIWA, FROM THE HILLS BEHIND TENNENJI	64
AZALEAS ON THE ROCKS, TENNENJI	65
THE POEM	67
WHITE AZALEA BUSH, RAKU-RAKU-TEI, HIKONE	69
THE BAMBOO GROVE, TENNENJI	71
SUNSET OVER LAKE BIWA, FROM TENNENJI	75
PLANTING RICE	77
A SPRING FLOWER—JIRO-BO	78
PLATYCODON GRANDIFLORUM, "KIKYO"	80
AURATUM LILIES AND BOCCONIA ON THE HILLS NEAR NIKKO	82
A FIELD OF LILIES, OFUNA, NEAR KAMAKURA	83
SEVEN BEAUTIFUL FLOWERS OF LATE SUMMER	85
HYDRANGEA BUSH, TOTSUKA, NEAR YOKOHAMA	87
UNDER THE CRYPTOMERIAS AT NIKKO	89
A LITTLE TEMPLE AT NIKKO	91
KIRIFURI, NEAR NIKKO	93
THE MOOR NEAR YUMOTO	94
A WET DAY AT CHŪZENJI	95
THE FOOT OF NANTAI-ZAN	97
THE MOAT OF BENTEN-SHIBA	99
SPECTATORS	104
THE LAST TEA LEAVES—COTTAGE NEAR YOKOHAMA	105
LOTUS-PONDS AT KAMAKURA	107

	PAGE
LOTUS-PATCH AMONG THE RICE-FIELDS, KAWASAKI, TŌKYŌ	109
A TEA-HOUSE AT KAMAKURA	110
YORITOMO'S WILLOWS AND HIS SHRINE	111
JAPANESE WRESTLERS	113
LESPEDEZA "HAGI"	115
THE HEART-LEAVED LILY	116
CAMPANULAS ON FUJI	118
GOING UP IN THE MIST	121
A CLOUDY EVENING, FROM THE SANDS OF TAGO-NO-URA	123
FUJI FROM THE ABEKAWA, AND THE TOKAIDO BRIDGE	124
ON THE NORTHERN SLOPE OF FUJI—GRASS-CUTTERS RETURNING	126
THE SECOND SHELTER IN THE GOTAMBA PATH	128
FUJI WITH ITS CAP ON	130
FUJI FROM THE KAWAGUCHI LAKE	131
FROM THE TOP OF FUJI, LOOKING NORTH	133
THE GREAT PALM AT RYUGEJI, FUJI IN THE DISTANCE	135
THE CRATER OF FUJI	136
AN OLD RED PINE AT YOSHIDO	139
NAKA-NO-CHAYA, ON THE NORTHERN SLOPE	143
THE RED-PINE GROVE AT YOSHIDA	145
FUJI OVER THE RICE-FIELDS OF SUZUKAWA	146
THE FLOWERY MOORLAND	147
TAIL-PIECE	150
THE AUTUMN LILY	152
FIELDS NEAR HAMAMATSU	154
THE EDGE OF THE TOKAIDO, NEAR HAMAMATSU	155
THE ISLAND OF AWAJI, FROM MAIKO	158
ON THE SHORE NEAR MAIKO, THE STRAIT OF AKASHI TO THE RIGHT	159
LILIES BY THE SHORE, SUMA	160
A GRAVEYARD AT SUMA	161
HILLS BEHIND KŌBE	162
A BAMBOO-YARD AT MAIBARA	163
BLUE WATER-WEED	164
THE TRAVELLING THEATRE AT MAIBARA	165

	PAGE
LAUNCHING A BOAT	168
LAKE BIWA WITH FLOODED RICE-FIELDS, NEAR MAIBARA	169
ONE OF THE "YAMA" AT THE NAGAHAMA MATSURI	173
SOME HATS AT THE NAGAHAMA MATSURI	174
THE TEMPLE GARDEN, SEIGWANJI	175
MINIATURE PAGODA IN THE TEMPLE GARDEN, SEIGWANJI	177
A CHRYSANTHEMUM SHOW AT YOKOHAMA	179
THE ARSENAL GARDEN, KOISHIKAWA, TŌKYŌ	183
TAIL-PIECE	185
LYCHNIS GRANDIFLORA, MISAKA-TOGE	186
TRICYRTIS HIRTA, ATAMI	188
TAGO-NO-URA	191
COTTAGES AT NEMBA	192
LAKE SUWA AND THE NAKASENDO MOUNTAINS, FROM KAMI-NO-SUWA	195
TOURISTS AT A WATERFALL	199
NIEGAWA, ON THE NAKASENDO	201
A LITTLE SHINTO SHRINE, NEAR THE NAKASENDO	202
A BOAT-MENDER BY THE TENRYUGAWA	203
BANANA-TREES AT ATAMI	207
THE FERRY AT TOKIMATA	209
ON THE TENRYUGAWA	210
THE VILLAGE STREET, ATAMI—VRIES ISLAND IN THE DISTANCE	211
ON THE TENRYUGAWA, NEAR KAJIMA	213
AUTUMN-GRASS (SUZUKI)	215
A RUSTIC BRIDGE AT DOGASHIMA, NEAR MIYA-NO-SHITA	219
AVENUES OF TORII IN FRONT OF AN INARI TEMPLE, NEAR SHIMIZU	221
JIZŌ SAMA, NEAR HAKONE	223
TAIL-PIECE	226

THE JAPANESE SPRING

CHERRY-BLOSSOM BADGE, YOSHINO

THE JAPANESE SPRING

WE had left Hong-Kong enveloped in its usual spring fog, and for five long, weary days had steamed across the China Sea in regular monsoon weather, gray and wet and miserable, but during the fifth some rocky islands, outlying sentinels of the three thousand which compose the Mikado's realm, and occasional square-sailed, high-sterned boats, showed that we were near Japan, the Far East, the Land of Flowers and of the Rising Sun, the country which for years it had been my dream to see and paint; and by six o'clock in the evening, on the 9th of March, we were at anchor in Nagasaki Bay. The aspect of that port on a wet day was not inviting, nor were the little grimy girls, who in a chattering, laughing line carried their baskets of coal on board; so, difficult as it was to decline the hospitable invitations of the English residents, I decided to go on with the ship to Kōbe. Early in the morning of the 11th we passed through the Strait of Shimonoseki—the sun shining brightly on the snowy hills and on the crowd of fishing-boats which had been sheltering there from the bad weather—and entered the Inland Sea. After so many days of monotonous gray ocean it was delightful to steam along in sight of land, and wind about among the islets and rocks, so near to many of them that we could see the little villages, the mists of white plum blossoms, the rows of beans and barley growing wherever a level patch could be made on the steep slopes, the people at work in their

IN THE INLAND SEA

fields, and always in the distance the ranges of snow-covered mountains in Kiushiu and Shikoku, the islands which enclose this lovely sea on the south. I longed to land and begin work at once, with a nervous dread in my heart that I should find nothing so good elsewhere, and, indeed, though there is plenty of material to be found everywhere

HILLS NEAR KŌBE, FROM SUWA-YAMA

in Japan, I saw nothing finer than these islands of the Inland Sea; to cruise about among them in a comfortable boat would be an ideal way to spend a summer, and would probably not be devoid of adventure, for our captain told me many tales of treacherous currents and sudden squalls and sunken reefs.

We reached Kōbe next morning, and before I had been on shore more than an hour I had heard of a village six miles away which was celebrated for its plum orchards, and had started off to find it. Okamoto lies at the foot of the hills which rise behind Kōbe on the north, and climbs a little way up them, and in front of the highest cottage, a modest tea-house with platforms arranged to accommodate the visitors who come in crowds to gaze at the blossoms, I unfolded my stool and easel, and in spite of a bitter wind and vicious little snow-storms made my first sketch in Japan. All round me and in the village below were the pink-and-white trees, then a band of rice-lands, pale green with young barley, and beyond them lay Osaka Bay, and the mountains of Yamato, which constantly changed in color as snow-storms passed over, or gleams of sun lighted the shining water and the snow on the distant hills. It is an exciting thing to begin work in a new country, to compare the local color and the atmosphere with those you have tried before, and to find yourself half unconsciously using an entirely new set of pigments. I was too absorbed with these problems to take any notice of the fact that my back was aching, but after two hours, when I had finished my drawing, I found myself unable to rise from that sketching-stool, and for the next fortnight an attack of lumbago prevented my seeing anything more of the plum groves. The Buddhist pictures of their Inferno depict many ingenious tortures; I think they ought to add a man with lumbago doing six miles over a Japanese by-road in a jinricksha. When at last I got back to Okamoto there were still some blossoms, and the trees were tinged with the pink of withered petals, but the luxuriant freshness had gone.

On the 13th of April I said good-bye to my friends and to the comforts of the Kōbe Club, and started for Nara, stopping on my way at Osaka to have a look at the town and see the peach blossoms on Momo-Yama (peach mountain). The narrow streets leading up the hill were crowded with visitors, and among the orchards of dwarf trees temporary tea-sheds and resting-places had been erected for their comfort and refreshment. In spite of the many picturesque features in these fêtes the whole effect is at first disappointing: railings and stages of new raw deal, the untidy and unfinished look of rough bamboo structures, with corners of matting hanging loosely in places where they interfere with the perspective lines, the slovenly pathways,

EARLY PLUM BLOSSOMS, OKAMOTO, NEAR KŌBE

which are mud or dust according to the weather—all these things make unsatisfactory accessories for the figures and the flowers. After a time they obtrude themselves less on your notice, and you have learned to accept the fact that Japan is not a country of big masses and broad effects, but of interesting bits and amusing details. This is usually true of its landscape; the forms of mountains and trees are more quaint than grand, and the cultivated land has no broad stretches of pasture or corn, but is cut up into patches, mainly rice-fields, with various vegetables grown in little squares here and there.

It was as yet too early in the year for any rice to be planted out. In the fertile valley through which the railway runs from Osaka to Nara some new fields were lying wet or fallow, others were being prepared by spade labor, and others again, not yet flooded, were covered with the bright green of young barley, or the strong light yellow of rape in flower.

Though I had read much about life in Japan, it was an embarrassing experience to be set down for the first time with my baggage in a Japanese room, and to try and adapt myself mentally to the possibilities of living under such conditions. In a bare hut or tent the problem is comparatively simple; there is always one way by which you must enter; but in a Japanese room there is too much liberty; three of the walls are opaque sliding screens, the fourth is a transparent, or rather translucent, one; you can come in or go out where you like; there is no table on which things must be put, no chair on which you must sit, no fireplace to stand with your back to—just a clean, matted floor and perfect freedom of choice. European trunks look hopelessly ugly and unsympathetic in such surroundings, nor are matters much improved when the host, in deference to the habits of a foreigner, sends in a rough deal table, with a cloth of unhemmed cotton, intended to be white, and an uncompromising, straight-backed deal chair. These hideous articles make a man feel ashamed, for though they are only a burlesque of our civilization, they are produced with an air of pride which shows that the owner is convinced they are the right thing, and one cannot but be humiliated by their ugliness and want of comfort. Yet if you want to read or write you have to keep them and make the best of them, for a long evening on the floor is only to be borne after a good many weeks of practice. Things begin to look brighter and pleasanter when the little waiting-maid appears, bringing first some cushions and the hibachi, with its pile of glowing charcoal, and then the tea-tray and a few sweet cakes. This was more the sort of thing I had expected, and made me at once feel at home with my surroundings. It is the first attention shown you in every tea-house, no matter how humble; whether you go as an inmate, or whether you merely sit down for a few minutes' rest on a journey, the little tea-pot and the tiny cups are at once produced, and the hibachi is placed by your side, a pleasant and friendly welcome, which never failed to make its impression on me, however poor the quality of the tea might be. The Kiku-sui-ya (which means Chrysanthemum-water house) is near the entrance to the great Kasuga Park at Nara; just outside it the road passes under a granite torii flanked with stone lanterns, and winds up to the temple through an avenue of cryptomerias, with rows of lanterns on each side, which get closer and closer together as they near the temple buildings, and are so numerous that tradition says they have never been counted. There are booths here and there where pilgrims can rest and get a cup of tea, for pilgrimage in Japan is not made unnecessarily uncomfortable, and where the tame deer congregate to take the nuts and cakes which are sold

THE TORII OF KASUGA TEMPLE, NARA

for them to the passers-by. From early morning till nearly sundown this road is lively with groups of visitors. Nara is so near to Osaka that among them a sprinkling of men, mostly no doubt engaged in commerce, wore foreign dress, but the majority of the people were in their native clothes, and as I sat and painted by the road-side I could study the variations of Japanese costume—from that of the old peasant with his white or blue

OLD WISTARIA IN KASUGA PARK, NARA

leggings, straw shoes, big hat, and robe tucked into his girdle, his head shaved down the middle, and the back hair turned up in a queue in the ancient mode, to that of the gay young musumé with her rich silk kimono, gorgeous scarlet petticoat, broad obi, and black-lacquered sandals on her pigeon-toed, white-socked feet. The cryptomerias are good, but the old wistarias are the glory of Kasuga Park. The great Fujiwara family formerly owned or were patrons of the temple, and though it is now imperial property, their crest, the wistaria flower (*fuji no hana*), is still worn by the little girls who perform the sacred dance there, and all over the park the wistaria vines are allowed to grow as they choose, their great snaky stems writhing along the ground and twisting up to the tops of the highest trees.

One very wet day, when painting out-of-doors was impossible, I went round to see the sights of Nara—Kobūkuji with its pagoda and fine old statues, the great Buddha, the celebrated big bell, and beyond these the Buddhist temple Ni-gwatsu-dō, perched on a hill-side, the steps leading up to it lined with stone lanterns, little shrines, and booths for the sale of endless trifles. The platform surrounding this temple is supported in front by a scaffolding

THE PAGODA OF KOBŪKUJI, NARA

CHERRY-TREE AND LANTERNS, NI-GWATSU-DŌ, NARA

of beams, at the back it abuts against the hill, and from the heavy projecting roof which covers both platform and temple hang hundreds of bronze lanterns, votive offerings. Each of these had been appropriated by a sparrow; trusting to the sanctity of the spot, they had piled in all the rubbish they could find to make their nests; odd ends of straw and paper stuck out everywhree, showing that their stay in the East had not taught them tidy habits. I am sorry to say that their confidence was misplaced; a temple festival came round before their eggs were hatched, and the whole of them with their embryo families were ruthlessly evicted in order that the lanterns might be lighted.

The park at Nara is one of the few places in Japan where you can see real turf, and even there I was struck by the scarcity of ground flowers; there were plenty of scentless violets, some yellow and white dandelions, and in the damp ditches a little purple flower called jirobo by the country people, but there was nothing to compare with the masses of daisies, buttercups, and cowslips which make the English meadows so bright in the spring. Perhaps the mountain moorlands would have been as gay at that time as I found them later in the year; the fields are far too well cultivated for any weed to get a chance of flowering.

The earlier cherry-trees were in blossom by this time, and I lingered on, making studies of them, and learning Japanese words and ways from O Nao San, a young lady about twelve years old, who had appointed herself my special attendant and protector at the Kiku-sui Hotel. One night at the theatre I saw a modern farce, with a policeman, an old-fashioned Japanese gentleman, a Chinaman, and an Englishman as the comic characters. They were ridiculous and amusing, but when all the earlier incidents of the piece were narrated with conscientious realism in evidence before a magistrate the thing became monotonous, and struck me as faulty in dramatic construction. This was the only theatre I saw in Japan in which they had discarded the orchestra and chorus and other traditions of the old stage.

There is a modest little temple opposite Kobūkuji, which is visited by most of the pilgrims to Nara; in its court-yard is a pile of stones from which a stream of water flows, fed by the tears of the mother of Sankatchu, a sacrilegious man who killed some of the sacred deer, who was killed himself in consequence, and buried here by her. Day after day groups of visitors stand by the fountain, listening intently to the guide who tells them the pathetic story, and give their prayers and a few coppers to her memory. The family affections are strong in Japan, and the love between parents and children, and among the children themselves, is always pleasant to see. The little ones are never slapped or shaken or pulled about roughly; you may wander through the streets for days without hearing a child cry, nor do they often quarrel in their play. But it is possible to go too far, even in filial piety. There was a murder trial while I was in the country, and by the evidence it appeared that the prisoner's mother was blind, that the doctor had prescribed the application of a warm human liver, and that he, as he

THE WELL OF SANKATCHU, NARA

could find no other way to get the remedy, had killed his wife in order to restore his mother's sight.

In most forms of Japanese art the technique which is admired by native connoisseurs, and the associations connected with the subject represented, can only be understood by those who have studied Japanese methods and traditions, but the old wooden statuary has more in common with Western art, and often reaches a high point of realism. In the religious figures certain traditions had to be followed, and in looking at these this fact has to be remembered; the exaggerated anatomy, unnaturally fierce expressions, and arbitrary number of limbs often disguise their true merits; but in the portrait figures of daimios, priests, and abbots the treatment is both simple and dignified. Mr. Takenouchi, a sculptor to whom I had letters, was making admirable copies of the principal sculptures at Kobūkuji, which were to be exhibited at Chicago, and afterwards added to the collection of the Fine Art Museum in Ueno Park, Tōkyō. Among the old masters, Unkei, a sculptor of the twelfth century, is perhaps the most noteworthy; there is a mendicant ascetic by him in the Hall of the Thirty-three Thousand Kwannon at Kyoto, a lean old man, clad only in a few rags, resting on his staff and holding out his left hand for alms, which might rank with the work of Rodin.

On the 25th of April the cherry-trees were in full flower, and I left Nara for Yoshino, a village at the foot of Mount Omine, in Yamato, which has for centuries been noted for its cherry groves. Here the cult of the cherry blossom has its headquarters, and during the ten days or so which the blossoms last the little town is crowded with visitors. I was too late to see the place in its full glory; it stands at some height above the sea, and I consequently imagined that the flowers would be later than those at Nara, but the cherry which grows there in such quantities is an early species, and three days of wind and rain had covered the ground with pink petals and left very few of them on the trees in the celebrated groves. Fortunately there were still some flowery trees to be found in gardens and sheltered corners, and at this time of year it would be impossible to settle down in a Japanese village without finding plenty of subjects to paint. The cherry in the Yoshino groves has a single flower, pale pink in color; this is followed by another

CHERRY BLOSSOMS IN THE RAIN, NARA

kind with white blossoms, more like the European species. Both of these are wild, and from them the Japanese gardeners have raised many varieties, double and single flowered, some with the growth of the weeping-willow, and others with a spreading habit. The flowers vary in color from white to light crimson, and I noticed some young trees with large double blossoms which were pale yellow with a pink flush on the outer petals, like a delicate tea-rose.

SARA-HIKI-SAKA, NEAR YOSHINO—LATER CHERRIES

At the Tatsumi-ya, just by the remains of the huge bronze torii, which, until it was blown down by a hurricane, formed the entrance to the main street, I found a little suite of rooms built in the garden away from the rest of the house, and at once engaged them, in happy anticipation of quiet nights. These isolated rooms have some disadvantages, such as having to get to the bath and back on wet nights, but a very short acquaintance with life in a tea-house makes the traveller disregard such trifling inconveniences for the certainty of peaceful sleep. The Japanese wanderers usually finish their day's journey about five in the afternoon, and, after the preliminary cup of tea, discard their travel-stained clothes for the clean kimono which every well-regulated tea-house supplies to its guests, then bathe in water as near the boiling-point as possible, eat their dinner, sit talking and smoking till midnight, snore till five o'clock in the morning, when the clatter of taking down shutters begins, and the elaborate business of tooth-cleaning and tongue-scraping, with an accompaniment of complex noises suggesting sea-sickness in its worst stages, so it is not till they have departed at six or seven o'clock that a light sleeper gets much chance. In the daytime the tea-house is deserted, except by the proprietor, who sits in the front room and does his accounts, and by the little servant-girls, who, with their heads tied up in towels, kimono tucked into their obi, and sleeves fastened back, showing a good deal of round brown leg and arm, busily sweep and dust the rooms in preparation for the new set of visitors who will arrive in the evening. The thin sliding partitions would be little bar to sound even if they reached to the top of the room, and above them there is generally a foot or so of open wood-work, which allows free ventilation and conversation between the different apartments. Privacy, as we understand it, is no part of the scheme of a Japanese tea-house. Real fresh air from outside is very difficult to get at night. During the hot weather I was always careful to examine the fastenings of the wooden shutters with which, after dark, every house is enclosed like a box, so that I could surreptitiously open a crack opposite my room, although by so doing I was disobeying the

CHERRY AND LATE PLUM, TEMA-CHO, NEAR NARA

police regulations. These shutters do not keep out the noise of the watchman, who all night long wanders round and knocks two blocks of wood together, just to let burglars know that he is on the lookout.

In these quarters I spent a week or so, painting all day when the weather would allow me, and in the evening struggling with the language and gambling for beans with the family and the servant-girls, who played *vingt-et-un* (*ni ju ichi*) with such keenness and discretion that I was generally made a bankrupt, with much laughter and clapping of hands, quite early in the game, and had to be set up again by general contribution.

Everything in Yoshino is redolent of the cherry; the pink and white cakes brought in with the tea are in the shape of its blossoms, and a conventional form of it is painted on every lantern and printed on every scrap of paper in the place. The shops sell preserved cherry flowers for making tea, and visitors to the tea-houses and temples are given maps of the district—or, rather, broad sheets roughly printed in colors, not exactly a map or a picture—on which every cherry grove is depicted in pink. And all this is simply enthusiasm for its beauty and its associations, for the trees bear no fruit worthy of the name. There is an old Japanese saying, "What the cherry blossom is among flowers, the warrior is among men." I was reminded constantly of a sentence which a friend had written in one of my books, "Take pains to encourage the beautiful, for the useful encourages itself." It is difficult for an outsider to determine how much of this is genuine enthusiasm and how much is custom or a traditional æstheticism; but it really matters little. That the popular idea of a holiday should be to wander about in the open air, visiting historic places, and gazing at the finest landscapes and the flowers in their seasons, indicates a high level of true civilization, and the custom, if it be only custom, proves the refinement of the people who originated and adhere to it.

The village street of Yoshino winds up a spur of the hills, passing many temples and little hamlets, and gradually becomes a steep and stony mountain path, which ascends to Mount Omine. The great tracks of forest provide occupation for most of the people in this district; as I sketched by the road-side strings of men and women were constantly passing, carrying down heavy loads of wood and charcoal from the hills, and in front of many of the cottages match-wood was spread out on mats to dry. It was difficult to understand how it could ever get dry, for all the mists of Japan seemed to collect round these mountains and forests; the landscape was rarely free from them, and constantly looked like a Japanese drawing, all vague and white in the valleys, with ridges of hill and fringes of pine showing in sharp clear lines one behind the other.

It is a warm climate too, and everything grows luxuriantly. There are great clumps of bamboo, enormous azalea bushes, and thick undergrowths of palmetto. On the roadside banks in this last week of April, there were ferns just unrolling, the fronds of maidenhair (*Adiantum pedatum*) all bright-red young shoots of lily and orchid and Solomon's-seal, and a lovely iris (*I. japonica*), with many lavender-colored flowers on a branching stalk, each outer petal marked with dark purple lines, and decorated with a little horn of brilliant orange. The gardens of tea-houses and temples were gay with azalea, camellia, magnolia, and cherry, and with the young leaves of maple and andromeda, as bright as any flowers. During a great part of the year these gardens have but few blooms—they are only an arrangement of greens and grays — but in the spring no amount of clipping and training can prevent the shrubs from blossoming. The cherry-trees and magnolias are let

grow as they choose, but the others are trimmed into more or less formal shapes, considered suitable to the species, or helping the carefully studied arrangement of forms, which is the ideal of a Japanese gardener. There are no beds for flowers. In the little ponds the irises and lotus bloom, and in odd corners there may be clumps of lilies, chrysanthemums, or other plants, but these are mere accidents: the designer's aim is a composition of rocks, shrubs, stone lanterns, ponds, and bridges, which will look the same in its general features all the year round, and conform to established rules. One of my Japanese friends told me, as an instance of the complexity of the landscape-gardener's art, that if a certain shrub were used it would be necessary to place near it a stone from Tosa, the distant province where it commonly grows. The decorative garden is quite distinct from the flower garden, where the fine varieties of iris, pæony, and chrysanthemum, for which Japan is famous, are grown by professional florists, or by rich amateurs who can devote a special place to their culture.

On the 3d of May my host at the Tatsumi-ya brought me some pæony flowers arranged in an old bronze vase. This showed me it was time to move on to Hase, where there is a great display of them, so next morning I made an early start for a long jinricksha ride through the hills of Yamato. My baggage and painting materials could not be packed in less than two kuruma, two more were necessary for my boy and myself, and the four vehicles, with two men drawing each, made an imposing procession as we bumped down the steep village street. The whole staff of the Tatsumi-ya had turned out to say good-bye; there was a row of little girls kneeling on the floor, their noses on the matting and their brown hands placed flat, palms downward, in front of their heads, and the landlord, after giving me the usual presents and a receipt for my "chadai"—the parting tip—insisted on accompanying me to the end of the town.

Our route for two or three miles, as far as the river Yoshino-gawa, was the same that I had climbed on my way up; but nine days had made a great difference in its aspect. Then many of the trees were still bare; now they were covered with spring leaves. After ferrying over to Muda we turned northwards, and a good road led us by low passes and through the grand forests at the foot of

CROSSING THE FERRY AT MUDA, ON THE YOSHINO-GAWA

Mount Tonomine down to Tosa in the Yamato Valley. Jinricksha travelling is very pleasant when the roads are good, the weather fine, and the men active; there is no noise of horses' hoofs to disturb the mind, the straw-sandalled feet of the coolies hardly make a sound, nor is your attention distracted from the landscape by having to drive; and the frequent short halts at way-side tea-houses give you a chance of airing your few phrases of Japanese and seeing the ways of the people. My lunch at Tosa was en-

MI KOMORI JINJA, A SHINTO TEMPLE NEAR YOSHINO

livened by two charming waitresses, who had evidently seen but few foreigners, and who were much interested in me and my belongings. My watch, match-box, cigarette-case, and other small articles had to be examined, talked over, and shown to the rest of the household, and I was plied with questions about my age, my family, and other personal matters, as Japanese etiquette prescribes.

This valley of Yamato is the earliest historic home of the present race; in it there are many tumuli which mark the burial-places of legendary emperors, including that of Jimmu Tenno, the first of all, and it is therefore considered sacred ground by the ancestor - loving Japanese. Every year crowds of pilgrims walk over the district, making their "Yamato-meguri," or tour of the holy places of Yamato, and thereout the innkeepers suck no small advantage. Hase was full of them, and every tea-house crammed; in the room next mine at least a dozen must have slept, and I thought myself lucky to get a place to myself.

There were still some hours of daylight left after I had settled down in my quarters, so I wandered up the street and climbed the long flight of steps to the great temple of Kwannon. On each side of the steps small beds were built up, and in these the pæonies grew, and their big flowers, ranging in color from white to dark purple, glowed in the afternoon light against a background of gray stone lanterns. The temple is built on a hill-side, like Ni-gwatsu-dō at Nara and many other Buddhist temples, and it consists of a wide veranda filled with incense-burners and votive pictures and bronze lanterns, and of an inner sanctuary. Across the entrance to this stands an altar, and over it an opening in the dark purple curtains allows a glimpse of the great gold figure of Kwannon, nearly thirty feet high, her face, with its expression of calm beneficence, only just distinguishable by the light of a few dim lamps in the gloom of the window-

THE STREET, HASE

less shrine. Behind this main temple there are various other buildings, priests' houses and such like, and a little pond for the sacred tortoises.

The main street of Hase is cut up with rivulets; the middle one is used for all domestic purposes, and at all hours you may see the women, with skirts and sleeves tucked up, washing their clothes or their fish and vegetables, and ladling up water for baths and cooking with their long-handled wooden dippers. The side streams turn small water-wheels, which work wooden hammers for pounding and cleaning the rice—an important part of the day's work in every Japanese village. In the most primitive places it is done with a long-headed wooden mallet and the stump of a tree hollowed out for a mortar; in others big wooden hammers are fixed on a pivot, and are raised by stepping on the other end of the handle, tread-mill fashion. A mountain brook, the parent of these little streams, tumbles along close behind the houses; its banks are overhung with bam-

ANDROMEDA BUSHES IN KASUGA PARK, NARA

boos, and the rocks at that season were covered with clumps of lavender iris. From Atago-Yama, a hill just across the river, the view is fine; below are the flat, gray roofs of Hase, and the *cul-de-sac* in which it lies—bordered on either side with green hills, its windings indicated by the curves of road and shining river, its green surface spotted here and there with gray hamlets—gradually opens out into the wider Yamato Valley. Unebi-Yama, which marks the site of Jimmu Tenno's mausoleum, rises in the centre of the plain, and beyond it all is an enclosing barrier of cloudy mountains.

A morning's jinricksha ride took me back to my old quarters at Nara, and Kwannon must have rejoiced at my departure from Hase-dera, for while I was there most of the priests and all the acolytes sadly neglected her: they spent

WHITE WISTARIA, HASE-DERA

the day looking over my shoulder or gazing open-mouthed in my face. This was on the 9th of May, and I was glad to find that the wistaria in Kasuga Park was just in its glory. The masses of flowers turned the lower trees into big bouquets of pale mauve, and seemed to drip like fountains from the tall oaks and cryptomerias; and to add to the beauty, all the undergrowth of andromeda had put out its young leaves in many shades of color; as Chaucer says, "Some very red, and some a glad light green." One glade particularly attracted me: a tiny clear stream wound along through the brilliant grasses, and the trees which covered the steep banks on each side of this little meadow were completely overgrown with the vines, and smothered with their blossoms. This too was a quiet spot, out of the track of tourists and pilgrims, and it was a blessed relief to work without a gazing crowd; the only passers were a few women and children collecting firewood or gathering the young fern shoots which were sprouting through the grass. These are cut just as they begin to unroll, and when they are boiled and flavored with soy, they are really quite good to eat, at least one thinks so in Japan.

The wistaria blossoms were almost gone when I decided that though there was still plenty to be done in Nara, it would be better to try some new sketching-ground, and having heard of a tea-house with a fine old garden at Hikone, on the shore of Lake Biwa, I determined to move on there for my next venture. I packed all my belongings, and made arrangements for the journey next morning, and then walked once more round the park and the temples, gazing regretfully at all the good things which still remained to be sketched, and climbed Mikasa Yama, a steep grassy hill behind the park, which on fine days is dotted all over with picnic parties. From its summit there is a great view over the plains round Nara, with the Kizugawa, a good

A TALL WISTARIA, KASUGA PARK, NARA

broad stream, winding through them. The grassy ridges and the few wind-beaten pines which grow on them made a fine foreground, and the little green gullies were spotted with low azalea bushes covered with flame-colored flowers. It was too good to leave, and I ought to have unpacked again and prolonged my stay for a few days; but laziness prevailed, the bore of repacking seemed intolerable, and to my lasting remorse this subject remained unpainted.

NOTES AT MUDA

BADGE OF THE KIKU-SUI-YA

EARLY SUMMER IN JAPAN

IRIS JAPONICA

EARLY SUMMER IN JAPAN

IT is difficult nowadays to imagine how the Japanese managed to live without tea; everybody drinks it at all hours of the day, and the poorest people rarely get a chance of drinking anything stronger, and yet it is, as things went in old Japan, a comparatively recent introduction. Tea was introduced with Buddhism from China, and though some plants were brought as early as the ninth century, it was not much grown until the end of the twelfth. Daruma, an Indian saint of the sixth century, often represented in Japanese art either crossing the ocean on a reed, or sitting a monument of patience, with his hands in his sleeves, was the father of the tea-plant. After years of sleepless watching and prayer he suddenly got drowsy, and at last his eyelids closed and he peacefully slept. When he awoke he was so ashamed of this pardonable weakness that he cut off the offending eyelids and threw them on the ground, where they instantly took root and sprouted into the shrub which has ever since had power to keep the world awake.

In the twelfth century Kyoto was the centre of life in

CARRYING HOME TEA LEAVES, NEAR UJI

Japan, and the district of Uji, between that city and Nara, has always kept its reputation for producing the finest tea. The most valuable leaves are those on the young spring shoots, and when I passed through on the 19th of May these were just being gathered and dried. Most of the shrubs grow in the open air without any protection, evergreen bushes from two to three feet high, and among them the women and children were at work. As they squatted by the plants, filling their baskets, very little of them was visible, but their big grass hats shone in the sun, looking like a crop of gigantic mushrooms. The Japanese "kasa" is made of various light materials — straw, split bamboo, rushes, or shavings of deal; it is used, like an umbrella tied to the head, as a protection against sun and rain; in the evening or on cloudy days it is laid aside, and the laborers wear only their cotton kerchief, spread out like a hood, or tied in a band round their brows. Though it cannot be called the "vast hat the Graces made," it is, nevertheless, very effective in the landscape, and the variations of its outline in different positions indicate happily the action of its wearer.

The plants which produce the most expensive teas, costing from six to eight dollars a pound, are carefully pro-

A PLANTATION COVERED WITH MATTING NEAR UJI

tected by mats stretched on a framework of bamboo, so that the tender leaves may neither be scorched by the sun nor torn by the heavy rains, and there are acres of them so enclosed. It was a curious thing to look down from a little hill-top on a sea of matting which filled the whole valley from one pine-clad hill to another, its surface only broken by the ends of the supporting poles and by the thatched roofs of the drying-houses which stuck up here and there like little islands. Underneath the mats women were picking, and in every wayside cottage those who were not in the fields were busily sorting and cleaning the leaves. There are no large factories or firing-houses; each family makes its own brand of tea, labelling it with some fanciful or poetic name, such as "jewelled dew."

The road through this fertile district crosses two large rivers, the Kisugawa and Ujikawa, and many smaller streams. They are all carefully banked in, and the water is carried where it is needed by endless ditches and channels. During the heavy rains these rivulets become raging torrents, and would soon cover the country with stones and gravel if they were not kept under control; the quantity of débris they bring from the mountains is so great that, instead of being down in a hollow, they are raised above the rest of the country, and you have to go up-hill to ford them. Before getting into the long and uninteresting suburbs of Kyoto there are some large ponds on either side of the way, willows and tall reeds growing on their banks, and in every little creek fishermen with their boats and nets, all very picturesque and paintable. So was the Nesan at the Tatsu-ya, who when I halted for lunch at once led me round to the principal room at the back of the house (the best rooms and the gardens are usually at the back), and showed me her tame gold and silver carp, which came to be fed when she clapped her hands. It was a tiny little

POND IN THE GARDEN OF RAKU-RAKU-TEI, HIKONE

garden, not more than twenty-five feet square, but it had its pond and bridge, and mountain of rock, and old pine-tree, like the best of them.

I reached Hikone by rail the same evening, and took up my quarters at the Raku-raku-tei tea-house, a great rambling place, with a large garden and suites of rooms to suit all tastes. I was shown into a gorgeous apartment with gold screens, its floor raised above the level of the rest of

THE CASTLE AT HIKONE

the house, which no doubt was intended for great people, who in the old days must often have come here to see the Daimio, Ii Kamon no Kami; but I felt I could not live up to this, and after viewing the rooms overlooking the lake, and those built on piles over the fish-pond, I selected some that looked out into the garden, with a trellis of wistaria just in front under which the purple trails of blossom nearly a yard long were still hanging. There are no crowds of

THE CASTLE AT NAGOYA, FIELD OF IRIS IN THE FOREGROUND

visitors now, and the fine old garden looks rather tangled and neglected, with bushes untrimmed and paths overgrown with weeds. On a steep rocky hill close by is the castle where the Daimio formerly lived; the hill is on one side protected by the lake, and on the others by a wide moat, crossed by picturesque wooden bridges, and the roads which lead to the plateau at the top are defended by more bridges over dry moats, gate-houses, and zigzag walls of large, well-fitted stones. The architecture of all these castles is very much alike, and though there are not many of them now standing, they must have abounded in the feudal times. The finest I saw was that at Nagoya; it was a good deal shaken by the last great earthquake, but is still quite sound, and the great gold dolphins on its bronze roof shine high above the rest of the city. In the short period after the introduction of Western ideas, when the craze for things European

AN OLD CASTLE MOAT, AKASHI, NEAR KŌBE

led to many acts of vandalism, most of them were pulled down, and this one at Hikone was only just saved from destruction by the intervention of the Emperor; now that a reaction has set in, and the Japanese official mind is not so eager to forget the past and obliterate its relics, they are likely to be carefully preserved. All of them have a massive foundation of large stones, not squared except at the angles, but carefully trimmed and fitted together without mortar; and the superstructure is of timber and plaster, with roofs and eaves of heavy tiles or metal. The moats, overhung with pines and filled with lotus during the summer months, are always interesting. It was a blazing hot day when I walked

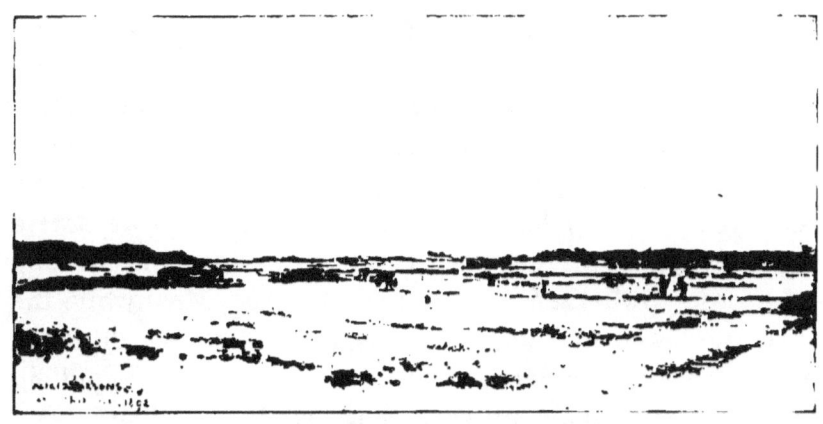

FIELDS NEAR LAKE BIWA

up and examined the castle; there was not a cloud in the sky, and Lake Biwa and its mountains lay still and clear and soft in the delicate blue haze which seems to be their own peculiar property. The fields outside the town were covered with a bright pink flower like a clover, which is not used for fodder, as there are hardly any animals to feed, but is dug in to improve the land for the rice, and this blaze of color consoled me for not finding as many azaleas as I expected. I set to work at a study of it, and sent my boy Matsuba, who, with the quickness of his race, quite understood the kind of thing I was looking for, to search the neighborhood for azalea bushes. He came back early in the afternoon to tell me that he had not been successful, but that there were some races going on in the town, so we wandered up, and established ourselves in a room just over the starting-post. The course was about two hundred and fifty yards along the pebbly bed of a dry river, and all the arrangements were very unlike those of a European race-course. Two upright posts of bamboo stood about five yards apart, with a stout pole slung between them; the vicious little ponies were brought along by two grooms, each holding a long cord fastened to the bridle, and with a good deal of shoving and hustling were wedged in, shoulder to shoulder, between this pole and another behind them at about the height of their hocks. Their heads were pulled over the front pole, and held firmly by a groom with a long running cord through the bridle rings, while the jockeys were fully occupied in preventing the little brutes from striking each other with their fore and hind legs. Meanwhile the spectators, who had kept at a respectful distance until the ponies were safely fixed, crowded up behind them, pulling their tails and whacking them with bamboos. The starter then appeared, made a few remarks, and beat a small drum, upon which the men in charge of the pulleys dropped the front pole, the grooms slipped their ropes out of the bridle rings and jumped aside, and the ponies scrambled off as best they could. The jockeys rode without saddles or stirrups, with their great toes hitched into a surcingle, and directly they were off they dropped the reins, held their left hands in the air, and plied their whips with the right until they had passed the winning-post. It was just a scurry, with no time for scientific riding, and, as far as I could see, the pony who got over the pole best always won. O Kazu San, my waitress at the Raku-raku-tei, was helping at the tea-house, and kept me supplied with tea and cakes, and I stayed watching the races and the spectators, and being watched by them, until the dusk put a stop to sport. I left too soon, for my boy told me that there was a fight afterwards about a bet; it was the only fight I heard of while I

O KAZU SAN

was in Japan, and I should have liked to see it. Two days of heavy rain turned the course into a river once more, so that the heats were never decided. Some few days after, Matsuba told me that there was a "Japanese man's circus" in the town. It was not in the least like a circus; it was a theatrical performance in which all the members of the company, who in this troupe were women, were mounted on horseback. There was a small stage, with a set scene at the back, and in front of it, on the same level as the spectators, a space of bare earth on which the action took place. The play consisted mostly of combats; the swords and other necessary properties were brought in by attendants, and placed on a high stand where they could be easily reached by the actors, and the horses were then led into position, and held there while the fighting went on. None of the performers fell off, but beyond this there was no horsemanship; they could not even get their steeds on and off the stage without the help of a groom.

My thoughts recurred to another travelling theatre, at Stratford-on-Avon, where I saw a stirring drama called *Tel-el-Kebir, or the Bombardment of Alexandria*, in which Sir Beauchamp Seymour had a hand-to-hand conflict with Arabi Pasha. Mr. Lawrence, the spirited actor-manager, informed me afterwards, when I congratulated him on the performance, that it was always popular, and that he had played it twenty-three times in one day at Nottingham Goose-Fair. In reply to my objection that it took at least an hour, he said that of course they cut the dialogue, and only had the combats and the bombardment. I remembered, too, his remarks when called before the curtain at the end of his season; he enlarged on the dignity of the actor's profession, and how essential it was that he should be a gentleman, saying, in conclusion; "'Ow, I harsk, could a chimney-sweep (if there's a chimney-sweep present I beg 'is pardon), but 'ow could 'e act the part of a prince or a nobleman? 'E could not do it, my friends; 'e's not 'ad the hedjucation."

The fine days at this season were perfectly glorious; hot enough to give an inkling of what it would be like in the full blaze of summer, and yet with a taste of spring's freshness left in the air. They were interspersed with too many

PREPARING THE RICE-FIELDS

wet or uncertain days, but, with the garden close by, I managed to waste very little time. The first lotus leaves were just coming up in the ponds and the irises blossoming round the water's edge, the azalea bushes were covered with flowers, and the tips of the pale green maple boughs were tinged with rosy pink. When the pouring rain had begun to drip through my sketching umbrella, and I was driven in-doors, there was no lack of society. O Kazu San, a plain little thing with brown velvet eyes, and the rest of the girls were never tired of looking at my belongings, thumbing my sketch-books, and asking me endless questions; and though I was sometimes irritable, their good-humor was unlimited. This unvaried good temper is itself annoying, when the foreigner feels that it is not the result of sympathy, but because he is regarded as a strange animal, not to be judged by the rules which govern the conduct of civilized people. At last Matsuba told me that he had found a place, "top side," with plenty of azaleas, and rooms where I could stay. It was a small Buddist temple called Tennenji, once very popular but now almost deserted, which stood on the hillside beyond the rice lands, and somewhat above the swarms of mosquitoes which haunt the marshy shores and the lagoons of Lake Biwa. Ji means a Buddhist temple—at least

MY ROOMS AT TENNENJI

BUDDHA AND HIS DISCIPLES, TENNENJI

that is one of its meanings—and tennen means "produced by nature." The name itself suggested peace and quietness and repose, and these I found in that delightful place, always seen in my mind through a rosy haze of azalea blossom.

A granite sign-post where the little temple path turns off from a track through the rice-fields tells all who can read it that the temple is dedicated to the five hundred Rakkan (disciples of Buddha), and their gilded and lacquered effigies sit in long tiers round one large building within the court-yard; beyond this is the Hondo, where the principal altars are, and where the services are performed at daybreak by the old priest who has sole charge of the establishment. My room was a little annex of the Hondo, quite apart from the living-rooms of the family, and open on two sides to the air. The angle of my veranda projected over the fish-pond, and on the right and the left stepping-stones led down from it into the garden, a small patch of level ground, with a pine-clad hill-side rising sharply beyond it. Just at the foot of this hill there was a rocky projection, covered with an undergrowth of azaleas, and spotted with statues of Buddha and his sixteen principal followers. These were rudely carved of the natural stone; with their growth of lichens and mosses they looked as old as the rocks themselves, and were hardly to be distinguished from them at a little distance. Several stony zigzagging footpaths, mere tracks through the bushes and pine-trees, led to the top of the ridge, from which one looked down on fertile valleys enclosed by more pine-clad ridges, and to the westward on the great shining plain of Lake Biwa, its lagoons, islands, and distant mountains. Many times I walked to the top of this hill, sometimes in the clear brilliant moonlight, when the delicate pinks and reds of the azaleas were hardly visible, and only their honeysuckle scent made me conscious of their presence, and when all the world would have been silent but for the incessant chorus of myriads of frogs which came up from the rice-fields below.

In the daytime the whole of the wood was lively with cicadæ, who kept up a constant and irritating clatter, but then there was the delight of finding new flowers, or making the acquaintance of old garden friends in their own homes. A little damp gully just behind the bamboo grove was full of deutzia bushes in blossom, and under them grew a clump of pale pink lilies (*Lilium krameri*), which seemed

HIKONE AND LAKE BIWA, FROM THE HILLS BEHIND TENNENJI

to me the loveliest flowers I had ever seen. The priest at Tennenji was so anxious to have some of my work that I made a drawing of these for him; it hangs among the temple treasures, and may be a surprise to some wandering foreigner, who will little expect to find any European traces in such an out-of-the-way spot. The family, consisting of Sokin the father, O Shige San the mother, and Takaki, a son employed in the office of police at Hikone, soon

AZALEAS ON THE ROCKS, TENNENJI

adopted me as a friend, and did all they could to make me comfortable. Takaki had received a modern education (they teach English in the Hikone schools, as you find out from the small boys, who shout A B C after you in the streets); but he had not got beyond the word "Yes," beginning every sentence with it and then lapsing into Japanese. We made many excursions together, he, Matsuba, and I, strolling down to the town after dinner and looking in at the theatres and shops.* O Shige San was great at cooking, and took delight in providing me with new and strange forms of food every evening; for breakfast and lunch I ate what European food Matsuba could provide, and as flour and whiskey could be bought, and a cow was slaughtered in Hikone every Saturday, I did not do badly; you can get the necessary sustenance in a shorter time on foreign "chow," but when work was over and I had taken my hot bath and exchanged my suit of flannels for a cotton kimono, it was amusing to sit on the floor and speculate on the composition of the dishes which she brought me, trying with the aid of a dictionary to find out what they really were, and to acquire a taste for "dai-

THE POEM

* Before I left Tennenji he wrote in one of my sketch-books the poem inscribed above in Japanese characters. The reading is, "Yukuri no midzu-umi no fukaki kokoro wa chiyomo chigiran," and it ₁ughly translated thus: Deep as the water of Lake Biwa, my ⊔ ₄s been ever true and changeless since chance brought us together.

kon."* Among her successes were eels cooked in soy, broiled fish, and bean curd "à la brochette"; young bamboo shoots, chrysanthemum leaves fried in batter, and lily bulbs boiled in sugar were eatable; but a sausage made of rice and herbs, and some of the quaint vegetables, were simply nauseous. In one of my water-colors there was a large group of leaves, round ones with a dark hole where the stem goes in, commonly known as the "foreground plant," and I noticed one afternoon to my disgust that these had been cut; the boiled stalks were given to me at dinner that evening, and I never tasted anything more unpleasant. When the various dishes had all been brought in and arranged round me by the priest or Takaki, O Shige San would appear and kneel in front of me, keeping my sake cup and rice bowl filled, and watching with intense anxiety my expression as I tasted each compound, and at the end of my dinner would remark that I had eaten nothing, and that Japan was a dirty, ugly country, to which I always replied that I had feasted, that England was dirty and ugly, but that Japan was a beautiful country. Such is

---

* "Daikon" is a large kind of white radish, which is boiled and cut in strips and served as a savor with every meal; it is very tough, and both the smell and the flavor are repulsive. A well-known Yokohama poet has written some verses on the subject, which show a great knowledge of culinary French, and a rooted dislike to the vegetable which is shared by most foreigners. It commences in this way:

Cook loquitur (*gently*).
    Won't daikon do
    To stew
    With carrots and a bean or two?
    Methinks 'twould give a savor rare
    To cutlets à la Financière.
    Won't daikon do?
Master (*decisively*).
    No—daikon will *not* do!

Oriental politeness. Then Sokin came in with his pipe and pouch and little fire-box, and, after taking a cup of sake with me, sat and smoked and conversed, or brought out the tea things of his lamented patron, Ii Kamon no Kami, and made me a bowl of powder tea with all the correct ceremonies. The Cha-no-yu is not to be confounded with ordinary tea-drinking. It is an elaborate form of entertainment which cannot be appreciated by an uneducated foreigner; every movement is regulated by laws known to the initiated, and the conversation is confined to some object of art, or poem produced by the host. The kettle, water-bowl, and other utensils should all have some historic or artistic interest, and the cup from which the mixture is drank is usually an example of archaic pottery. The rules of the game have not been altered for about two centuries, though there are various schools which differ as

WHITE AZALEA BUSH, RAKU-RAKU-TEI, HIKONE

to minor details—whether the whisk with which the drink is stirred should afterwards be laid on the seventh or thirteenth seam of the matting, and things of that sort, which seem of infinitely small importance to the ignorant, but make a vast difference to the connoisseur. Our love of tobacco was a great bond of sympathy, although after trying each other's pipes we both preferred our own. The old man, who knew that I did not like to be watched while painting, would sit in his little room and gaze at me as I worked in the garden or among the stone gods on the hillside, and when he saw that my pipe was out, would fill another for me and bring it out with a box of matches, making this an excuse to look over my shoulder for a few minutes, and to have a little conversation.

As the summer came on and the weather got hotter the insects became more and more numerous; there were splendid butterflies and dragon-flies in the daytime, swarms of fire-flies over the rice-fields at night, and unfortunately many others which bit at all hours, flying things, and things which mosquito-curtains could not keep out. The Japanese house has no separate rooms for living and sleeping; when bedtime comes quilts are brought in and laid on the floor, and, if necessary, a mosquito-netting of thick green gauze is slung over them from the four corners of the apartment. The natives use a small wooden pillow, with a depression for the neck to rest in; I never could manage this, but after a time I succeeded in sleeping well with coats or another quilt rolled up for a bolster.

Certain paragraphs about me in the local papers brought a good many visitors to the temple to see what I was doing, among them a gentleman who was introduced to me as the best singer in Hikone, and a little conversation and whiskey induced him to give me some specimens of his art —songs of the Buddhist and Shinto priests, and others

THE BAMBOO GROVE, TENNENJI

which might be described as popular airs. To foreign ears they were quite devoid of melody, and his elaborate vocalization only produced sounds which were disagreeable and harsh, or else ludicrously inadequate to the efforts they cost him. My friend, who appeared to be an all-round æsthete, spent a good part of the afternoon in arranging a big bronze jar of azalea boughs and a hanging vase of irises, curling the leaves and snipping off any stray shoots which did not conform to the fish-scale arrangement (sakana no uroko no kata) which he was trying to make.

The family were very busy all through this month with their crop of silk-worms, which required incessant care and feeding. I was taken to see them first in an outbuilding when they were just little black specks; as they got older the air of this shed did not suit them, and they were moved into the Hondo, where they flourished and grew with astonishing rapidity under the eye of the Buddha, and devoured the baskets of chopped mulberry leaves as fast as they could be prepared. The caterpillars were huddled together on mats hung one above another in a framework; a netting of string was spread over each mat so that the whole mass could be lifted and the débris cleared away with very little trouble. When they had ceased to grow, and began to stand on end, waving their heads in the air after the idiotic fashion of silk-worms who want to spin, they were picked off and put in little nests of straw or bundles of brush-wood, which soon became a mass of soft yellow cocoons. It was an anxious time for O Shige San, for a considerable part of her income depended on the crop of silk; the cocoons are worth about thirty yen a koku, a measure rather less than five bushels.

The pond under my veranda was full of carp and baby tortoises, which hurried up to be fed as soon as they saw me leaning over the rail; the old tortoises were more shy, and I only saw them on very hot days, sunning themselves on the stones, and they slipped into the water with a flop if I attempted to get near them. I caught one on a patch of sandy ground, after watching its struggles to cover up the hole in which it had just laid some leathery-looking white eggs. These days brought out the snakes too, some of them very big, and all unpleasant to look at, but quite harmless. There is only one venomous snake in the country, a small brown beast called "Mamushi"; the other sorts are not ill-treated, indeed, they are considered lucky, but this is always killed and skinned, and a medicine is prepared from its dried body.

It would have been easy to dream away months here, but the wise regulations of the Japanese government, foreseeing that the traveller might be tempted to neglect his duties and become a mere loafer, forced me to return to Kōbe and get a new passport, so I had to say good-bye to my friends, and the Rakkan with the lichen-covered azaleas, still gay with crimson flowers which trailed round their feet, and the terrace where every evening I had watched the sun setting over Biwa, and to descend once more to the railway and the commonplace.

The rain came down in torrents as I left the temple, and continued to do so all the day, but there was plenty that was amusing to be seen from the carriage window. The people were busy putting out their young rice plants, and the fields were full of men and women working in mud and water half-way up to their knees, and wearing their "kasa" and straw coats, oiled paper, rush mats, or other contrivances to keep off the rain. It is surely the dirtiest and most laborious form of agriculture; the work is almost entirely done by manual labor with a spade and a heavy four-pronged rake, though I occasionally saw a cow

or a pony, with a little thatched roof on its back to shoot off the rain, dragging a sort of harrow through the mud. As soon as the spring crop of barley or rape-seed is garnered and hung up to dry, the ground is trenched with the spade, and water is turned over it until it has become a soft slush, which is worked level with the rake. The young rice plants, grown thick together in nursery patches, are pulled up when the fields are ready for planting, their roots are washed, and they are tied in bundles, which are thrown into the mud and water; then the men and women wade in, untie a bundle, and set the seedlings in lines by just pressing them with their fingers into the mud. They do this wonderfully quickly, and can plant eight or nine in a row without moving from their places; when the field is all planted it looks like a pond with a delicate green haze over it. The dividing banks are planted with beans or other vegetables, so that not a yard of ground is wasted. This was the 18th of June, the beginning of the " dew month," a period full of discomforts for the traveller, and especially for the landscape-painter.

PLANTING RICE

A SPRING FLOWER—JIRO-BO

THE TIME OF THE LOTUS

PLATYCODON GRANDIFLORUM, "KIKYO"

THE TIME OF THE LOTUS

THE damp heat of the Japanese summer, which is so trying to human beings, encourages all vegetation to grow with surprising luxuriance and rapidity; the buds of yesterday are flowers to-day, and to-morrow nothing is left but the ruin of a past beauty, making the painter's struggle most arduous just when he has least energy to contend with nature. The young bamboo shoots come up like giant asparagus, growing so fast that one can almost see them move; some of them are cut and eaten while young and tender, and those which are allowed to grow to large poles are used for every imaginable purpose. They are made into water-pipes and flower-vases, barrel-hoops and umbrellas, baskets and hats, scaffolding-poles and pipe-stems, fans and delicate whisks for stirring the powdered tea—more things, in fact, than I could enumerate in a page. The bamboo is surely the cause of much of the clever constructive work of the Japanese; for though it will do most things with proper treatment, it will not stand being handled like ordinary timber; its peculiar qualities have to be considered, and every way in which they use it is artistic and good. This is the large species which grows to twenty or thirty feet high; there are many dwarf kinds, which clothe the hills with green, and are used only for making fences and such like.

The general aspect of Japan during the summer months is a harmony in greens, the dark pines and cryptomerias striking the lowest note of a scale which culminates in the

AURATUM LILIES AND BOCCONIA ON THE HILLS NEAR NIKKO

A FIELD OF LILIES, OFUNA, NEAR KAMAKURA

brilliancy of the rice-fields — the most vivid green I know. There is more variety of color in those districts which are not irrigated, such as that round Kamakura, where the light sandy soil grows a great many kinds of vegetables, sweet-potatoes, melons, tomatoes, beans, and big patches of auratum and longiflorum lilies, the bulbs of which are exported. The lily is not one of the flowers which the Japanese themselves particularly admire, nor do they often use it for decoration. In this, as in most other matters, there are recognized rules of taste, and the man is con-

SEVEN BEAUTIFUL FLOWERS OF LATE SUMMER
1. Susuki 2. Kikyo 3. Asago 4. Shion 5. Omnia-Meshi 6. Kiku 7. Hagi
Drawing by Toshoto Hario

sidered an ignoramus who does not know the right thing to like. I was walking one day at Yoshida with a Japanese artist, a remarkable man who was engaged in making a series of steel-engravings, half landscape and half map, of the country round Fuji, and called his attention to a splendid clump of pink belladonna lilies growing near an old gray tomb; but he would not have them at all, said they were foolish flowers, and the only reason he gave me for not liking them was because they came up without any leaves. When we got back to our tea-house he took my pen and paper, and showed me what were the seven beautiful flowers of late summer—the convolvulus, the name of which in Japanese is "asago," meaning the same as our "morning-glory;" wild chrysanthemum; yellow valerian; the lespedeza, a kind of bush clover; *Platycodon grandiflorum*, a purple-blue campanula; *Eulalia japonica*, the tall grass which covers so many of the hills; and shion, a rather insignificant-flowered aster. I noticed that some versions of the seven flowers differed from his; a large-flowered mallow is often substituted for the last he named. There are doubtless different schools which hold strong views on the subject, but on the morning-glory and some others they are evidently agreed. The auratum lily is a common wild flower in the hilly districts, and boiled lily bulbs are a favorite vegetable, but I could not find out which was considered the best variety for the table. O Shige San told me that it was a red lily; I looked in vain for any of that color in their gardens.

The cottages in the country round Kamakura are thickly thatched, and on the top of the thatch is laid a mass of earth held together by iris plants, which form a roof-crest of spiky green; near them in July there often were large hydrangea bushes covered with balls of blossom, the young flowers a pale yellow-green, changing as they grew older through bright blue to purple.

On the 9th of July the heat drove me from Europeanized Yokohama to the hills. I left the train at Utso-no-miya, a little town which has been financially ruined by the railway —for every one formerly stayed a night there instead of travelling straight through—and was delighted to find myself once more in thoroughly Japanese quarters. It was a wonderful moonlight night, and I wandered round the town in kimono and clogs, watched the people, and was stared at by them, climbed the steps to the big Shinto temple, and

HYDRANGEA BUSH, TOTSUKA, NEAR YOKOHAMA

UNDER THE CRYPTOMERIAS AT NIKKO

gazed over the plains flooded with pale light, and thoroughly enjoyed myself.

There is a railway now to Nikko, and most people rush up there without seeing the glorious avenue of cryptomerias —described so well in Loti's *Japoneries d'Automne*—which line the old road for miles and miles. I sent my boy and my baggage by rail, and went myself in a kuruma with two good runners. The road is sadly out of repair in some places, but the splendid old trees remain, and young ones have been planted where winds and age have thinned their ranks. It is not like an ordinary avenue with the trees planted some yards apart; these are so close together that the trunks have often joined at the base, and I noticed one lot of seven big trees all grown together at the bottom into a mass that must have been eight or ten yards long. The road is sunk between the high banks on which the trees grow, and it must be gloomy enough on such a night as Loti experienced. Here and there it opens out into a village street, with abundance of refreshment booths for the pilgrims who still make the journey on foot.

Nikko itself is a long, steep street, leading up to a rushing mountain torrent in a rocky ravine, which is crossed by two bridges side by side. One is an ordinary wooden structure, used by all the world; the other, which is of red lacquer, with black supports and brass ornaments, is only opened for the Emperor and his family to pass over. Beyond them the hills rise, covered with cryptomerias, among which are concealed the great mortuary temples of Ieyasu and Iemitsu, founders of the great Tokugawa Shogunate that lasted for two centuries. Marvellous as these mausolea are, they make no effect in the distance; it is only when you get close to them, wander about in their successive court-yards, and examine the lovely details of wood-carving, lacquer, and gilding, that the wonder of them strikes you. The tombs themselves are plain bronze pillars, and are reached by long flights of granite steps, green and gray with mosses and lichens, which lead up under the dark masses of foliage behind the temples. After passing through all the glories of color and elaborate workmanship in the preliminary temples their final peacefulness and simplicity are very striking.

Nikko in the summer is full of foreign ladies and children; the Emperor, too, has a country-house there, where some of his large family spend the hot months. I saw the arrival of two little princesses, with a crowd of nurses, tutors, and officials. They were funny little things, about three or four years old, not as pretty as most Japanese children, but dressed in the most gorgeous colors. The red lacquer bridge was opened for them, decorated with "gohei"

A LITTLE TEMPLE AT NIKKO

—the strips of white paper which are used so largely in the Shinto religion—and in the middle of the bridge there was a little table with offerings of food on it, where the children stopped and made their obeisances to the manes of their ancestors as they passed over. All the priests of Nikko turned out in gauze vestments of many colors, Buddhist and Shinto equally anxious to do honor to the descendants of the gods.

The hills are alive with little tinkling streams of clear water, and the favorite walks mostly lead to waterfalls. I

KIRIFURI, NEAR NIKKO

THE MOOR NEAR YUMOTO

spent a soaking day making a sketch of one of them—Kirifuri; the path to it crossed a wide, stony river, and went over grassy hills where there were abundant wild flowers, purple iris, white and mauve funkias, yellow orchids, clusters of white roses, pink spiræas, hydrangeas, St.-John's-wort, meadow-rue, and bocconia appearing here and there, half hidden among the rank herbage. The big buds of auratum lilies showed how fine they would be in a few days' time. Just in front of the waterfall a little tea-house gave me shelter enough to work in; but the path, up which I had walked dry-shod, by the time I got back had been turned to a raging torrent, and I only just crossed the stony river in time, for the light bamboo bridge was washed down during the night.

Chūzenji is a little hamlet, some hours' walk from Nikko up a mountain road, consisting of a group of tea-houses which overlook a charming lake, a very sacred temple with a large bronze torii, and long rows of sheds to accommodate the pilgrims who come in early August to make the as-

A WET DAY AT CHŪZENJI

cent of Nantai-zan, the mountain which rises close behind
the village. During five long days of incessant rain I painted
everything that was visible from my room in one of the tea-
houses, the water of the lake rising each day so much higher
that on the last two I was able to take a morning header
from my balcony, and I hardly got a chance to explore the
country round. At last a bright morning tempted me to

THE FOOT OF NANTAI-ZAN

walk on to Yumoto, and see the sulphur springs and the
wide moorland, Senjō-ga-hara, which lies surrounded by
mountain-peaks at a height of nearly five thousand feet
above the sea. On the moor the grasses do not grow high
enough to conceal the flowers, and I found it gay with purple iris and white meadow-rue. The baths in Yumoto are
open to the public; they are large wooden tanks under

sheds by the road-side, and as you walk along the street you see the patients, men, women, and children, all sitting together, in a state of nature, up to their necks in the steaming malodorous soup. The clouds were gathering round the mountain-tops as I started to walk back to Chūzenji, and before I had finished a rapid sketch on the moor the rain began again in torrents; the road was a series of small ponds, and my coolie insisted on carrying me, as well as my sketching materials, through them; but he unfortunately stumbled under my weight, and dropped me in the deepest of them, and what with the wet above and below I was well soaked by the time I reached my tea-house. The hibachi seems a very inadequate means of warmth on such occasions; a hot bath and whiskey and dry clothes are more effective, and after dinner a bottle of tamago-sake, a hot compound of whipped egg and sake, soon produces a pleasing drowsiness. Since leaving Chūzenji I have recognized the place in many drawings on screens and fans; the artist always gives its main features—the lake, the cryptomerias, the huge bronze torii, and the steep wooded slope of Nantai-zan—but he combines them in one view as you never can see them in reality. The rain had played havoc with the road back to Nikko; several bridges were down, but temporary ones built of fagots made it possible to cross the streams. All the higher woods near the lake are hung with gray moss, and the flowering shrubs which grow among them are endless—azaleas, climbing and bushy hydrangeas, weigelia, seringa, and wild vine; on the ground I found orange Turk's-cap lilies, columbines, the big *Lilium cordifolium*, and ferns of many kinds.

Notwithstanding the advantage of cooler nights, I was glad to leave the green mountains, with their constant rain and mists, and the shut-in valleys, where it was impossible to see more than a few hundred yards away, and get down

THE MOAT OF BENTON-SHIBA

again to the broader horizons and bigger skies of the plains. On the journey to Tōkyō I saw my first lotus flowers in a lake near the railway, and I hurried off at once to the pond which surrounds the little temple of Benten at Shiba, where I found them in full glory.

The lotus is one of the most difficult plants which it has ever been my lot to try and paint; the flowers are at their best only in the early morning, and each blossom after it has opened closes again before noon the first day, and on the second day its petals drop. The leaves are so large and so full of modelling that it is impossible to generalize them as a mass; each one has to be carefully studied, and every breath of wind disturbs their delicate balance, and completely alters their forms. Besides this their glaucous surface, like that of a cabbage leaf, reflects every passing phase of the sky, and is constantly changing in color as clouds pass over.

Japanese drawings of flowers—and they usually draw them beautifully—are often influenced in some way by a tradition. The man who invented the method was a true impressionist; he seized what appeared to him characteristic of the plant, and insisted on that to the exclusion of other truths, thus founding a mannerism which all following artists imitated. In time, what he saw as characteristic became exaggerated by his disciples, who looked at nature only through his eyes and not with their own, and I have observed that the flowers which are most frequently drawn are not depicted so naturally as those less popular ones, in books of botany and such like, for drawing which there is no recognized method, and where the draughtsman had to rely entirely on his own observation for his facts. Take, for example, the spots on the lotus stems; if you look very closely you can see that there are spots, but certainly they could not strike every artist as a marked feature of the plant, for they are not visible three yards away. But some master noticed them many years ago and spotted his stems, and now they all spot them, and the spots get bigger and bigger; and so it will be until some original genius arises who will not be content with other people's eyes, but will dare to look for himself, and he may perhaps, without abandoning Japanese methods, get nearer to nature, and start a renaissance in Japanese art.

The Japanese treatment of landscape is not more conventional than that of Claude or David Cox, or than the shorthand of our pencil-sketches, but it records its facts in a different way. The everlasting question in art is the imitation of nature; it has never been carried further in certain directions than by Millais and his pre-Raphaelite brethren, or in others than by Manet, Monet, and the modern French, but no one can put in everything; look at a simple bunch of leaves in sunlight against a wall, and think how long it would take to really imitate all their complexities of form, color, and light and shade; some facts can only be given by ignoring others, and the question what is the important thing which must be insisted on is the personal affair of each individual artist in every country where art is unfettered and alive. But in Japanese, as in Byzantine and other Eastern arts, this question is still decided by the practice of past generations, and it will take all the vitality of a strong man to infuse new life into it without destroying its many exquisite qualities. Perhaps when Japanese artists absorb its spirit instead of merely trying to imitate its methods, Western art may help in the direction of freedom; at present I fear that its influence has done more harm than good.

The people are so quick to recognize the meaning of a few lines, and to understand the poetic idea which they suggest, that it is a wonder the artists ever learned to draw at all; they might have been content with symbols, for a few lines like those below are enough to convey all the poetry that is associated in their minds with any of the well-known art motives.

The little island of Benten is a frequented spot, and my easel was surrounded from morning till night with a crowd of spectators; they dispersed at the command of the policeman on his hourly round, but after he had gazed his fill and left me, a new lot instantly assembled. They were mostly children; and a crowd of Japanese children is twice as many as any other crowd of its size, for every child has another smaller one tied to its back. I suppose they are not born in pairs this way, but they contract the habit of carrying a little one at a very early age, and often tie on a doll when a sufficiently small human being cannot be found. The spectators are almost always polite, and take care not to put themselves between you and your subject; but they squeeze up very close to your elbow, and trample on your nerves, if not on your materials. They usually remarked that my work was a photograph; some more educated ones said that it was an oil-painting, that being the medium which is associated with foreign art; and one man said that it was enamel, which I took as a compliment to the brilliancy of my color. The keeper of a little tea-shed hard by, where I took my lunch, noticed that I was worried by the people standing so close to me, and when I arrived next morning I found that he had put up a fence round the place where I worked; it was only a few slender bamboo sticks, with a thin string twisted from one to another, but not a soul attempted to come inside it. They are such an

SPECTATORS

obedient and docile race that a little string stretched across a road is quite enough to close the thoroughfare. It is difficult to reconcile the character of this peaceable and pleasure-loving race which the modern traveller sees with that which is ascribed to their forefathers—those heroes of the desperate wars and bloody revolutions which fill the pages of the early history of Japan. It may be that two centuries of Tokugawa rule, fatherly but autocratic, developed qualities of unreasoning obedience, and perhaps all the struggles of the past were merely dynastic, or affairs between the warriors of different clans; perhaps the people themselves have always been as gentle as they are now, cultivating their land and pursuing their ingenious trades, little affected by these turmoils, except that, like the producers of all times and countries, they were called on to supply the sinews of war.

The lotus is intimately connected with Buddhism; most personifications of the Buddha are represented as seated or standing on its flower, or holding an unexpanded bud in their hands; it is largely used in temple decorations, and

THE LAST TEA LEAVES—COTTAGE NEAR YOKOHAMA

vases with imitations in metal of the flowers, leaves, buds, and seed-pods, often very exquisite in workmanship, stand on all the altars. It is typical to the Buddhist mind of the qualities of the ideal man: as it grows in the mud, yet produces a lovely flower, it is a symbol of purity in a naughty world; as its odor sweetens the air around, so his good deeds influence those about him; it opens in the morning sunshine, and his mind is expanded by the light of knowledge; its branchless stalks, rising without a break to the leaf or flower, are a type of his single-mindedness and directness of purpose; and its edible root shows that the basis of his life must be usefulness to others. To this I may add that, like the very good, the flower always dies young. It is lovely enough in itself without all this halo of virtue. Hardy says of Tess, "Beauty to her, as to all who have felt, lay not in the thing, but in what the thing symbolized"; this is unavoidable with most of us, and the suggestion of feelings and memories of our own does not necessarily obscure our visual sense; but a fixed and recognized suggestion is the result of mental laziness, and may lead to the ignoring of intrinsic beauty; as our lovely primrose is to some eyes a political badge, admired only because of its association with a name and a faction, or rejected for the same cause. To quote Mr. Punch,

> "A primrose by the river's brim
> A party emblem was to him,
> And it was nothing more."

But the lotus has not sunk so low as this; though it has been adopted by the Buddhists, it excites no animosity in Shinto breasts; and where temples under the present *régime* have been handed over from the one religion to the other, though the pagoda and other distinctively Buddhist

LOTUS-PONDS AT KAMAKURA. ALFRED PARSONS.

structures are pulled down, the lotus-ponds are left in their beauty. The largest I saw were those connected with the great Hachiman temple at Kamakura, which has been turned over to the state religion; they cover several acres, and the flowers in them are of three colors—either white, bright rose, or a delicate shell-like pink. All three varieties seem to grow equally freely, and one is as lovely as the other. The white one has been specially adopted by

LOTUS-PATCH AMONG THE RICE-FIELDS, KAWASAKI, TŌKYŌ

the followers of Nichiren, a noisy sect which beats a drum during the long hours of prayer, and it is this variety, too, which is usually grown in patches here and there among the rice-fields for the sake of its roots. They have not much flavor, except that of the sugar with which they are boiled, but they are crisp in texture and pleasant to munch. The children are very fond of the nutlike seeds which are

A TEA-HOUSE AT KAMAKURA

embedded in the fleshy seed-pod; it looks very like the rose of a watering-pot. In the tea-booths round the temple of Benten they use a dried slice of this pod for a mat on which to stand the cup or bowl.

Kamakura was for a long time the capital of Japan; in the twelfth century it was selected for his headquarters by Yoritomo, the great warrior whose victories enabled him to take the reins into his own hands, and to establish that system of military government which only ended with the deposition of the last Shogun in 1868. But when a rival family defeated his successors they removed the seat of government, and Kamakura rapidly declined from a great city of more than a million inhabitants to the insignificant fishing-village which it now is, with nothing to show of its former greatness but this temple of Hachiman, and the Daibutsu, an enormous bronze Buddha, not only remarkable for its size, but also for being the finest and most dignified production which the art of Japan can show. The temple buildings which once sheltered it were destroyed ages ago, and the image is now in the open air, in one of the little valleys which branch out from the plain and run back among the pine-clad hills. Centuries of exposure to rain and sun have given varied colors to the great bronze god. He is seated cross-legged on a lotus-flower, his hands folded in his lap; the head is bent slightly forward, and his face gazes down with an expression of calm superiority which can only come from perfected wisdom and subjugated passions. A new shrine to Yoritomo's memory, all of black and gold, stands near one of the lotus-ponds; in front of it are some splendid old willow-trees, which he is said to have planted, and under which he sat and composed poetry when he was not engaged more actively in fighting. It is hardly possible that these willows can have lived to such a great age; they are probably descendants of the original trees. Behind the shrine is a large modern barrack, and I saw bands of white-clad recruits, with side-arms and repeating rifles, trousers, tu-

YORITOMO'S WILLOWS AND HIS SHRINE

nics, and forage-caps, quite European in everything but face and stature, constantly passing to and fro over the ground where the old warrior must have seen his quaint soldiers in lacquered armor and bronze helmets carrying their long-bows and queer-shaped halberds. One day when I was painting the willows my boy Matsuba, who had plenty of spare time for investigating the neighborhood while waiting to carry home my umbrella and things, came and told me that there was a wrestling-match at a small temple about a mile away. I packed up at once and we walked over there, for I was very anxious to see what kind of a sport it was. This was a tournament, and all the professional wrestlers of the neighborhood, and many youths anxious to distinguish themselves, had collected to take part in it. They were divided into three classes. The masters of the art were all past their first youth; not enormously stout, as they are often represented in drawings and carvings, but fine, athletic men, taller than the average of Japanese. They wore their hair in the ancient style, shaved away from the centre of the head, and the locks from the back and side made into a queue, turned up and knotted with a string on the top of the poll; they had no clothes except a loin-cloth and an embroidered apron. In the second class were men who had won but few prizes; they were not all in the professional get-up, and some of them were evidently laboring-men with a taste for sport. The third class was composed of youths, none of them more than nineteen or twenty years old. The contests took place in the temple court-yard on a circular bed of sand, under a roof supported by wooden pillars, but not enclosed at the sides; round the edge of this raised circle there was laid a straw rope, and the man won who could either fairly throw his opponent or force him across the rope without being dragged over himself. The proceedings were conducted by a Shinto priest in full dress, wide trousers, and a coat sticking out from the shoulders like that of a modern young lady, who with a peculiar-shaped fan gave the signal to begin and to stop. For the highest class this umpire was a venerable old gentleman; for the others the place was taken by young priests who needed to learn this part of their business. The wrestlers came on in pairs as their names were called, and after a great deal of marching round, stamping, rubbing their limbs, making gestures of defiance, and so on, they squatted opposite each other. When the

JAPANESE WRESTLERS

signal was given to begin they rested their fingers on the ground between their knees, and leaned towards each other till their foreheads touched, sometimes waiting several minutes before attempting to make any grip. If the grip seemed unfair or unsatisfactory to one of the opponents, he immediately put down his hands, the priest stopped the bout, and all the preliminary business had to be gone through again; but if it seemed all right the struggle began, and sometimes lasted for five minutes, each man straining every muscle in a splendid way, and using all the science and cunning he knew. If it lasted too long without either man gaining any advantage, the priest signalled to them to stop, and they had to wait till their turn came round again. The preceding rough sketch, made while jammed in the crowd of spectators, will give some idea of the attitude of the men waiting for the fan to be lowered. Everything was conducted in the most ceremonious and orderly manner, and there was no drunkenness or rowdyism, although the multitudes who had assembled were entirely of the poorest class. The most fashionable wrestling-matches are held in Tōkyō in spring and autumn, and the champion is as much a popular favorite as a famous torero in Spain, or a well-known prize-fighter in England and America.

Those who read these notes will have gathered that the heat and the rain make summer life in Japan not wholly enjoyable; let me also say some words of warning to the thin-skinned against the mosquitoes, and even more against a horrible little insect which lives in the grass or sand and bites your legs and feet. It is so small that I never succeeded in finding it, but its bite brings up a blister which breaks and leaves troublesome sores. There were few nights from June till October when I was not obliged to get up once or twice and bathe them in cold water to allay the intolerable itching. The sea, too, has its terrors. I went down to the shore near Kamakura one hot night, hoping that a swim would soothe my troubled skin, but no sooner had I plunged into the approaching wave than my neck and arms were embraced by jelly-fish, and I scrambled out feeling and looking as if I had taken my bath in a bed of nettles. The Japanese, although they grumble and fan themselves a good deal, do not really mind the heat; their draughty houses are admirably adapted for fine summer weather, and their clothing is sensible and scanty. But the foreigners suffer, and as September comes, and the lotus flowers fade, they hail with relief the approach of the cooler and dryer weather of autumn.

LESPEDEZA "HAGI"

THE HEART-LEAVED LILY

FUJISAN

CAMPANULAS ON FUJI

FUJISAN

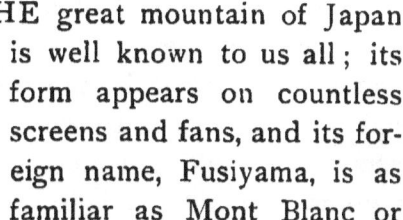

THE great mountain of Japan is well known to us all; its form appears on countless screens and fans, and its foreign name, Fusiyama, is as familiar as Mont Blanc or Pike's Peak. By the Japanese it is called Fuji, or Fujisan, or sometimes Fuji-noyama when speaking poetically: it is difficult to understand how an *s* came to be substituted for the *j* by foreigners, but under any name there is a peculiar fascination about the mountain, and the first sight of it, from the hundred steps in Yokohama, from Ueno in Tōkyō through a haze of telephone wires, or across the waves of Suruga Bay from the deck of a steamer, is an event which will be fixed in the traveller's memory

I can never see a high place without wishing to be on the

top of it, and Fuji looks obtrusively high. The long sweep with which it heaves its twelve thousand feet above the shore, the absence of any competitive mountains, and the exaggerated perspective of its broad base and narrow summit, all add to this impression, and the ambitious soul longs to be on such a superior eminence. And there is no better way of taking a holiday than to climb a mountain. To go down a river leads to laziness; things glide by which look as if they ought to be sketched, but to do so would involve stopping the boat, and interfering with the forces of nature which are gently furthering the traveller's ends, and thus the mind is tossed to and fro between the delight of seeing things and the unpleasant feeling that it is a duty to work. Thinking is the one thing to be especially avoided on a holiday, and there is too much time for thinking on an ordinary river. The same objection holds against walking on easy roads; in fact, the farther you walk the more you think; but in climbing a really big hill all thought is killed for hours by the simple physical exertion, and you become a mere machine, with a laboriously pumping heart and very heavy legs. And what a sense of superiority comes when the highest point is at last reached, when the world is all below you, half cloud and half solid earth, lovely, mysterious, and absolutely unpaintable. Even this sense fades from me in a few minutes, and I become a nonentity, with only a vague feeling of the hugeness of the universe and the infinitesimal smallness of the individual, and the opening verse of Adam's morning hymn always comes into my mind, as it did years ago on the top of a Somersetshire hill overlooking the Glastonbury flats, just after my first reading of "Paradise Lost."

An artist often hears the remark, "You must find painting a great resource," as if it were an amusement like golf or trout-fishing; and no doubt to many people a landscape-painter's life seems like one long holiday; but the struggle with ever-changing skies and fast-fading flowers has its fatigues, and the mind gets wearied of constantly thinking how this and that ought to be painted, so when a friend in Yokohama suggested that we should go up Fuji together, I accepted his proposal with alacrity, and we chose the first week in August for our excursion, that being the time when there is the best chance of good weather, and when most pilgrims are to be seen on the mountain. One of the most boring things in life is to walk through new and interesting country with a man who has no eyes for anything but his watch, and who insists on telling you how many minutes the last mile has taken; but my friend's figure was a sufficient guarantee against any attempt at "record-cutting,"

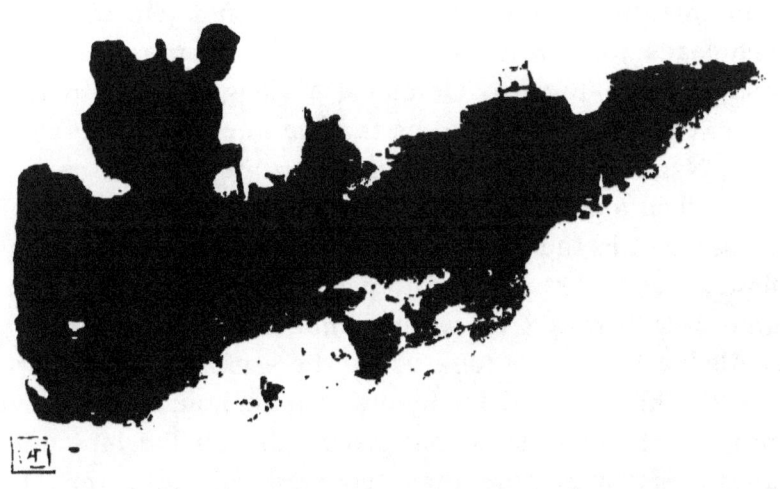

GOING UP IN THE MIST

and I felt sure that his pace would give me plenty of time for looking about.

The weather for our start was not promising—that damp summer heat of which there is so much in Japan, heavy and depressing, shrouding the mountains from morning till night in dense masses of cloud, which seem to slowly drag themselves up from the valley, and never succeed in getting clear of the hill-tops. From Miya-no-shita to the Hakone Lake we were from time to time enveloped in these clouds, and a thin drizzling rain prevented us from enjoying what in fine weather would be a very lovely walk. The moor at the northern end of the lake, Sengoku-hara, is dotted with herds of cattle, and is perhaps the only place in Japan where this familiar sight can be seen. You may wander for miles over the green hills and moorlands which cover so large a portion of its surface without ever seeing a four-footed animal; perhaps because the tall, coarse grasses and the leaves of the dwarf bamboos are unsuitable for fodder; perhaps because the Japanese are not a meat-eating nation, and do not need herds and flocks.

Our intention was to cross this moor, and join the road which leads from Miya-no-shita by way of the Maiden's Pass, Otome-no-toge, to Gotemba, a village at the foot of Fuji, but our coolie assured us that he knew a shorter road by the Nagao-toge, so we struggled up the hill-side on our left, reached a post which marked the top of the pass, and then stopped in the mist to consider which track we should follow. Suddenly appeared to us an aged man, whose venerable face inspired us with confidence, and by him we were led astray. He took us by the semblance of a path along the hill-top, and for about half an hour we plunged through wet grass up to our necks, the thick white mist hiding everything more than ten yards distant; then he confessed that he had lost his way, that he had heard of

A CLOUDY EVENING, FROM THE SANDS OF TAGO-NO-URA

that road, but had never taken it before, and that it was all grown over—an obvious fact; so there was nothing to be done but find our way back to the post, and try the wider track from which he had beguiled us. He was a cheerful old soul, seventy-four years of age, who had just walked to some hot springs about twenty miles from his home to take the baths for a couple of days because he suffered from rheumatism. Either it was a very mild case or the baths were marvellously efficacious, for he led us down the hill at a rattling pace, and went five or six miles out of his way to atone for his error, and to put us in the right road for Gotemba.

The mists reached far down the hill, and when we were at last free from them we looked eagerly for Fuji. There was the sea below us, with the great curve of sand, Tago-no-ura, bordering Suruga Bay, and the green slopes rising from it showed where our mountain must be, but at the height of about two thousand feet a straight bank of white cloud ruled off the landscape, and of the summit we could see no sign. The path led us along the hill-side, where men were cutting the rough grass, and loading it on packhorses; it wandered in and out of the dry gulleys, and over the intervening ridges, and at last, descending to the northward, brought us through cultivated fields to a tea-house near the railway station, where our baggage and provisions were waiting for us. Gotemba is on the Tōkaidō Railway,

FUJI FROM THE ABEKAWA, AND THE TOKAIDO BRIDGE

and is therefore a much-frequented place during the six weeks or so when Fuji is considered to be "open." It has been ascended at all seasons, the laborious walking through soft snow being the only difficulty, and the chance of bad weather the only danger; but except from the latter part of July to the beginning of September the numerous rest-houses are unoccupied, and the climber is obliged to carry all provisions with him.

There were plenty of pilgrims about, waiting to start on the morrow or just returned from the mountain, some washing their weary feet, others tying their big hats and long walking-sticks in bundles for the luggage-van, and all chattering incessantly. After dinner a travelling company entertained us in front of our tea-house with songs and dances. The band consisted of two samisen, a bell tapped with a stick, and bamboo castanets. The dancers were all little girls, from ten to fifteen years old, dressed in the ordinary long-sleeved kimono, and the movements of their bodies and slim little hands and limbs were full of grace and variety. Each performance was a mixture of song, dance, and dialogue, with instrumental accompaniment; the music was queer, tuneless, and often harsh to the European ear, but with the blood-stirring quality of all genuine national music.

Before daybreak next morning the whole house was stirring, and it was useless to hope for more sleep. Most of the pilgrims start early in order to get to the top by sunset, sleep there, and descend the following day, but we had decided to sleep two nights on the mountain, and were in no hurry. Our heavier baggage was sent by pack-horse to Yoshida, on the north side of the mountain, and three coolies went with us as guides and porters, carrying some extra clothing and the solid food which seems necessary for European stomachs. In the village street our strolling players were already wandering round, trying with some preliminary chords on the samisen to attract an audience. Daylight did not suit them, they looked draggled and discouraged, and it was difficult to believe that those dirty little figures shuffling along in the mud could ever have had any charm or grace of movement.

The path from Gotemba to the summit is one steady ascent over beds of old ashes. At first it is a very gentle rise; the lanes wind through the fields with various crops,

ON THE NORTHERN SLOPE OF FUJI—GRASS-CUTTERS RETURNING

and past cottages with hedges of pink and white hibiscus; but after a few miles it begins to get steeper, the ashes are less disintegrated, cultivation only appears in isolated spots, and there are large stretches of gray moorland varied only with bushes and wild-flowers. The mist still hung round us, there was no landscape to be seen in any direction, and if it had not been for the flowers and the ever-new and quaint figures on the road, this part of the walk would have been dull. Besides the regular pilgrims there were many men and women leading pack-horses, those on their way up carrying provisions and fuel for the rest-houses, and those coming down bringing bundles of grass so large that they looked like walking hay-stacks, and the wiry little ponies that carried them were almost invisible. In front a misshapen head peeped out, underneath were four thin little legs with enormous feet, and as they passed, their narrow drooping quarters, cat-hammed and cow-hocked, swayed at every step under the heavy load. Japanese drawings of horses have risen in my estimation since I have seen the models the artists have to work from; there never was a more ill-shaped beast than the ordinary horse of the country. In this as in many other hill districts mares only are used; they are shod with big straw overshoes, which give a finishing touch to their ludicrous shape; under them is slung a square of dark-blue cotton cloth to keep off the flies, and a narrow strip of the same material, with a big crimson cord and tassel printed on it for decoration, is draped across their quarters. Many of the pilgrims ride up as far as the tea-house called Uma-gaeshi (horse send back), and the ponies look almost as much eclipsed under the big pack-saddle with its trappings, and the pilgrim with his, as they do under the loads of grass.

When all cultivation had disappeared, and the road was a mere cinder track over a moorland of ashes, the flowers and bushes still grew in clusters here and there. The most abundant plant was a large bushy knotweed covered with sprays of white blossoms, and this grew far up the mountain-side. There were also clumps of tall bocconia, a campanula with large pink or lavender flowers sprinkled in each bell with tiny ink-spots, and various less showy flowers. The flora on this side of the mountain, devastated by the last eruption, in 1706, is not so rich as that on the northern slope. As the ascent became steeper we got into a wood of dwarfed and scraggy pine-trees, which extended as far as Tarōbō, a large tea-house with a little temple attached, and then suddenly ceased; above this there was only an occasional dead stump to break the monotonous surface of ashes. Here every pilgrim purchases a stick to help him up the mountain—an octagonal staff of birch, about five feet long, with an inscription burned on it, and for a few coppers the priests on duty at the summit will add a red stamp to prove that the owner has actually been there.

We reached the second shelter beyond Tarōbō quite early

in the afternoon; great masses of wet mist came constantly driving up the mountain-side; there was plenty of room in the hut, and nothing to be gained by going higher, so we decided to stay there for the night. All the regular tracks up Fuji are divided into ten portions, and a rest-house is supposed to mark the end of each division; but they vary much in their accommodation for travellers, and often get destroyed during the winter, so it is well to find out before starting which are habitable and which are not. Number Two (Ni-go-me), on the Gotemba path, was a roomy hut, built with blocks of lava; from below it looked like a wall with a hole in it, from above it was not visible, for the ashes covering its roof of rough planks were simply a continuation of the mountain slope; there was no chimney, but a mass of snow was piled over the fireplace, which dripped through the roof into a tub and supplied the establishment with water. By each shelter a small white flag fluttered on a pole to make its situation obvious.

Nothing could be more dreary than this spot on such an afternoon: above, below, and on each side the waste of

THE SECOND SHELTER IN THE GOTAMBA PATH

purple-gray ashes, light-green spots of knotweed and thistle, only enforcing the gloom of its color, seemed to stretch interminably into the mist, and nothing broke the monotony of the long oblique line except the little eminence of Hoei-zan, sticking up like a pimple on the great slope of Fuji, which occasionally showed its outline through the vague and formless clouds.

Inside it was, at any rate, warm; the raised floor was covered with coarse matting, and on this quilts were spread, and soon after dark we were all in bed. Some later arrivals had added to our numbers, and we slept thirteen in that hut, including the host and hostess; but this was nothing to the crowd at the top, where I think we were nineteen, perhaps more, for in some parts of the floor there must have been two or three under a quilt, and it was difficult to count them. Even here on Fuji you do not escape the all-seeing eye of the Japanese police; your passport is examined by the keepers of the hut, and is copied into a book which gives every night the names and addresses of those who sleep under the roof. About two o'clock in the morning we were wakened by our host, who took us outside, and there at last was Fuji itself, straight over our heads, every detail softened, but clearly visible, and the summit looking ridiculously near in the brilliant moonlight. Below us was the slope of ashes and the moorland over which we had walked; and in the distance the Hakone Mountains, already far below our level, lay half hidden by masses of moonlit cloud. More energetic men might have started at once for the final climb, but after gazing and shivering for a few minutes we turned into our hard beds again, and it was not till after sunrise that we left our hut, our party increased by a dreary and footsore young soldier in a soiled white uniform, and a cheerful coolie, carrying about a hundredweight of planks to repair one of the higher shelters.

The path goes zigzagging up to one rest-house after another, and there was not one of them which we failed to patronize; even Number Seven, which was a heap of ruins with nothing in the way of drink but a tub of melted snow, was an excuse for a few minutes' halt. In the clear morning sunlight Fuji looked small, as most mountains do when there are no clouds to give mystery and suggest height; but it was a grand morning for distant views, and the sunshine brought out vividly the strange and brilliant colors of the various materials which form the mountain—gray ashes, blue lava, and the reds and oranges of burned earth.

Above the seventh station the path turns to the left and passes behind Hoei-zan; already bands of pilgrims, who had seen the sunrise from the summit, were making their way back towards Gotemba, going at a great pace down the glissade of loose sand and ashes on its side, while we toiled on over harder cinders, with an occasional ridge of lava, on the upward path. At this altitude the knotweed and thistles had disappeared, and the only plants I saw were a dwarf

FUJI WITH ITS CAP ON

sedge and a little starwort in some of the sheltered nooks; higher still only a few lichens and mosses can grow; there is no regular alpine flora on Fuji.

A big gully full of snow lies just below Number Eight, and from this point the ascent is steeper than ever, winding among a chaos of shapeless blocks of lava; a sharp spur

FUJI FROM THE KAWAGUCHI LAKE

on our left crowned with them made a most curious outline against the sky. In front of us was a strange pilgrim, an old and feeble Buddhist priest in canonicals and a big cane hat; two coolies were hauling him by a cord round his waist, and another was pushing from behind, and even with this help he had to stop every few minutes to get his wind. He smiled a sickly smile as we went by; he was even slower than we were, and it seemed cruel to pass him; but he got to the top finally.

A sharp pull up a rocky gully at last brought us to a little wooden torii, and to the " Famous Silver Water," a clear, cold spring on the edge of the crater. The supply is not large, and the priest in charge of the enclosure doles it out to pilgrims at the rate of one brass cash for a small teacupful. The principal temple, and the cluster of huts round it, form a little square on the south side of the crater, just at the top of the Mura-yama path, and are reached from the Silver Water by means of a couple of ladders and a small fee. At the top of the ladders there is a tiny shrine, serving as stable to a toy model of a horse, and in front of this the coppers are deposited. There are only three entrances to the crater of Fuji, and each of these is marked by a small torii, the sacred gateway of the Shinto religion; two of them I have already mentioned, the third is on the north side, where the paths from Yoshida and Subashiri, which meet at Number Eight station, reach the summit.

Clouds had, as usual, begun to form about mid-day, and there were only occasional peeps of distance, but the crater itself was worthy of the journey, and occupied us until the bitterly cold wind drove us to shelter. Here, as on other mountains, I noticed that the first object of the native is to get under cover; all the kingdoms of the world and the glory of them may be spread before his eyes, but if there is a little smoky cabin, however rough and uncomfortable, the professional mountaineer goes inside and stays there. This one was not luxurious; near the doorway, the only aperture for admitting light, there was a smouldering wood-fire, where our food was cooked before we lay down to try and rest on the loose and creaky floor-boards; little blasts came like squirts of cold water through the cracks of the unmortared walls, and it was a relief when a general movement of the sleepers—for a Japanese can apparently sleep anywhere—showed the approach of sunrise.

The morning was clear and bright, and we all crouched in nooks of the rocks, wrapped in our quilts, and gazed at the straight gray line of the Pacific and the gradually brightening line above it, watching for the first sign of the approaching god. On the most prominent rock a priest knelt, waving strips of paper tied to a stick and chanting prayers and eulogies, and soon the sun rose, as he assuredly will every morning, whether he is prayed to or not. There

FROM THE TOP OF FUJI, LOOKING NORTH

was such a vast space of mysterious blue sea and distance below the horizon that the big orange ball appeared to be already half-way up the heavens when we first saw it. This daily occurrence seems ever new and wonderful, always has something of the miraculous about it, and to most minds it brings a sense of thankfulness, as the sunset gives that of repose; though why we should feel grateful both that it is time to begin to work and time to leave off is a puzzle to me. My thoughts turned to an early morning near Plevna, and to an honest Turk, who, as the sun rose over the bare Bulgarian hills, turned on his box-seat, and, gravely touching his forehead, wished a good-day to his "little brothers" in the carriage he was driving. There was a mixture of courteousness and solemnity in his manner which seemed exactly suited to the important moment.

When the orange glow had turned to a dazzling glare, we walked round to the foot of Kenga-mine, the highest of the peaks encircling the crater, and looked westward at the shadow of Fuji, a great pyramid of tender blue stretching for miles across the country at its foot, darkening a slice of the sunlit distant mountains, and towering above them into the sky, clearly defined on the light mists and clouds of the horizon. So sharp was the outline that it seemed as if our two shadows ought to show on the distant sky; but though we waved our arms frantically there was no visible movement on the edge; we were too small. When we returned to get some breakfast many of the pilgrims were saying their morning prayers at the little temple. "Sengen Sama" is the goddess of Fuji; a prettier name for her is "Ko no hana saku ya Hime"—"the princess who makes the blossoms of the trees to open." There is another little temple dedicated to her on the north side of the crater, and many more imposing ones in various parts of Japan. On a banner which floated in front of this second temple there was an inscription in Japanese, and under it these words in English, "Place for worship the Heaven." I suppose this was an effort in the direction of civilization and rationalism, but I resented it as an attempt to explain away the flower-loving princess, and to dethrone her from the mountain-top where she has been worshipped in peace for so many centuries. Close by the banner is another spring, "The Famous Golden Water," and a small shed, where bundles of chopsticks and other mementos are sold, and where for ten sen you can buy a tin can full of the famous water to take home to your friends. Most of the descending pilgrims have one or two of these tins slung round them with the rest of their travelling-kit. The regular Fuji pilgrim is dressed in a white tunic with loose sleeves, close-fitting white cotton drawers, white socks and gaiters, and a pair of straw sandals; he wears the usual big hat, which serves as an umbrella, and slung round his shoulders he has a light rush mat, which can be shifted to either side to keep off sun or rain. Round his neck he has a string of beads, a little incessantly tinkling bell, and a few pairs of extra sandals on a cord, and fastened to his waistband is the small package containing his personal baggage; he carries in his hand either the octagonal birch staff or a

THE GREAT PALM AT RYUGEJI, FUJI IN THE DISTANCE

THE CRATER OF FUJI

longer peeled wand, with some paper tied round the end of it. The dress of the women is the same as that of the men, except that they wear a short petticoat under the tunic, about as long as a Highlander's kilt. I saw none of them adorned with the bell and beads, so perhaps these are reserved for the men. It is only of late years that women have been allowed to climb the sacred mountain.

No one point of the crater's edge is high enough to give a panorama; you have to walk all round, about two miles, in order to see the view on every side. Eastward is the country round Yokohama and Tōkyō, with the Pacific beyond as horizon; southward, too, is the ocean, with the Izu Peninsula jutting out into it, and the sweep of Suruga Bay bringing it close under your feet; westward you get a glimpse of the Fujikawa River, with range after range of mountains behind it; and to the northward a chain of little lakes lies at the base of Fuji, these, too, backed up by mountains, which rise, one behind another, as far as you can see.

In some places the outer wall descends abruptly into the crater; in others, as by the Golden Water, there is a narrow plateau between the two. The crater itself is four or five hundred feet deep, the north side mostly precipitous rock, and the south side, under Kenga-mine, a steep slope of snow and débris; all the peaks round it have names, and one of them near the Silver Water is dotted with cairns raised in honor of Jizó, the patron saint of travellers, who helps little children to cross the Buddhist Styx. There is a rough path all round the crater, leading over some of the peaks, inside some, and outside others, which is kept in passable condition by men who collect a few coppers for their labor: the pilgrim season is harvest-time for the dwellers round Fuji, and its barren top pays well for cultivation.

It was after ten o'clock before we had made the circuit and seen all the sights; we met our coolies by the long row of huts at the top of the Yoshida path, and could see the village itself, our destination, lying in the blue hollow below us. Groups of ascending and descending pilgrims were visible for a long distance on the slope; as we looked down on them we saw only big round hats with an arm sticking out, and two little feet working underneath. After a final cup of tea at one of the guest-houses we passed under the wooden torii, and began the descent, a very steep and stony one, the loose cinders and lumps of lava requiring attention at every footstep. At Number Nine station there is a little shrine called "Sengen's Welcome," and at Number Eight there are six or eight good-sized huts built on a spur of harder lava, making quite a little village, which can be seen on a clear morning from the foot of the mountain. Here the Subashiri route branches off to the right; ours to Yoshida turned to the left, and we went sliding with long strides down an incline of loose ashes and sand, into which our legs sank up to the knee at every step. It was rapid but fatiguing, and required very high stepping to avoid heavy and ignominious falls. The track is marked by hundreds of cast-off "waraji"—straw sandals— a common object on all Japanese roads, but here especially plentiful. My companion had provided himself in Yokohama with a stock of them, specially made to fit over the European boot; they were carefully adjusted and tied on by our servants and porters, but I noticed that after the first hundred yards they had always worked loose, and after a quarter of a mile they were hanging gracefully round his ankles instead of protecting his feet. The enjoyment of walking depends so much upon foot-gear that I am shy of trying experiments, and I found that my stout boots with plenty of nails served as well on Fuji as on any other mountain. Worn as Japanese wear them, with a thong passing between the big toe and the next, the waraji hold on well; they are soon worn out, or made useless by the breaking of one of the strings of twisted grass which tie them to the ankles; but this does not matter, for new ones can be bought for about a half-penny at any road-side house. This part of Fuji was very desolate, the rocks were formless blocks piled up without any arrangement of line, and the débris was too loose for any plant to find a foothold; but after a few thousand feet a ridge of more solid lava rose on each side of the gully we were descending, and

AN OLD RED PINE AT YOSHIDO

that on our left soon began to show some vegetation. There were pines and larches, whose dwarfed and twisted forms showed the hardship of their lives, and among them were some flowers too, clusters of a delicate pink rhododendron, crimson wild roses, columbines, clematis, goldenrod, and orange lilies.

The glissade of fine ashes brought us down as far as Number Five station, and there we rejoined the upward path, for no one tries to ascend over this loose stuff. High up in the gully we had seen men digging out snow from under the ashes, and taking it across the flank of the mountain to supply one of the rest-houses on the ridge to our right, and troops of ascending pilgrims were visible now and then as a turn of their path brought them in profile against the sky. Below Number Five there is but one track; it plunges at once into a thick undergrowth of bushes, and after this we had no more desolate wastes of ashes, but a constant succession of trees and flowers, temples, and luxurious rest-houses, gay with the cotton flags presented to them by their patrons. The forest through which this path leads covers a steep ridge of lava; the trees are mostly pine and other conifers, often very fine old specimens, and under them is a tangle of flowering shrubs and plants and of fallen timber. The people we met coming up seemed to appear suddenly under our feet out of the green gloom; one party had always to draw aside while the other passed; at times the path was a stairway of old roots, at others a ditch between high banks, and never wide enough for two to walk abreast. We heard a sound of singing below us, and stood on the bank while about twenty white-clad pilgrims filed by, men of all ages, each with a little bell tinkling at his waist; the front ones chanted a short strain, which those at the back took up and answered, and their song was faintly audible in the woods above us long after the last had disappeared up the winding path. The chant is called "Rokkon shōjō"—the six senses purified—the six, according to the Buddhists, being eyes, ears, nose, tongue, body, and heart, and it is only sung by the Fuji pilgrims.

At Number Two station we made a long halt, emptied the ashes out of our boots, and washed our feet in the tubs of water which the little servants brought us. It was a very different kind of place from the rough shelter on the Gotemba side; the path came down a few steps as it emerged from the wood, passed under a torii by a small temple, and then spread out into quite a wide space in front of a long tea-house crowded with pilgrims. On the opposite side of this space were three or four platforms, spread with blankets and shaded with matting; these too were occupied by groups of guests, who smoked and drank tea as they rested, and below them the tops of the trees were cut away to give a space of open sky and a view of the distance. Hundreds of little flags were fluttering from long bamboo poles, and at the other end of this lively scene the path went down a few more steps, and became again a narrow track through the dense forest. The flowers all the way were abundant and beautiful, constantly varying as we descended from one zone to another; at last the wood became thinner, and we could get glimpses of the distance, and of the grassy ridges on each side of us, tinged with pale mauve by masses of funkia in blossom; and when we reached the temple and the large open square of the Uma-gaeshi we were at the end of the trees, and before us was a great slope of moorland leading down for miles and miles to the pine grove by Yoshida.

There is but one break in the long walk through flowers and grass—a little tea-house called Naka-no-chaya, whose three pine-trees are distinguishable for a long distance across the moor. All round it there are monumental pillars covered

NAKA-NO-CHAYA, ON THE NORTHERN SLOPE

with inscriptions, which look like tombstones, but were really erected by pilgrims to commemorate the number of ascents which they have made. The variety of plants which grow and flourish on this slope of fine cinders is truly remarkable. The most abundant flower was a pale mauve scabious, which gave a prevailing tint to the whole moorland, but the most conspicuous was a tall, slender day-lily

THE RED-PINE GROVE AT YOSHIDA

with a pale yellow flower, which shone like a star in the evening when the color had gone from all the others. A dark purple-blue campanula (*Platycodon grandiflorum*) was also very effective, and a bright crimson pink (*Dianthus superbus*) with beautifully fringed petals. But it would be hopeless to try and enumerate them. I find in a sketch-book a list of fifty-seven which I noted on the way between

Naka-no-chaya and Yoshida. A little later in the year this mass of flowers and grass is mown down and carried to the villages at the foot of the mountain.

The last part of our walk was through a grove of grand red pines, which seem to do better on this volcanic soil than anywhere else in Japan, and then across a few fields to the top of the long village street, where we at last found our tea-house and our baggage, and comfortable rooms, and settled down for a night of well-earned repose.

FUJI FROM SUZUKAWA.

Oct. 3, 1892.

Fuji is quite free from clouds this morning, and in the soft autumnal sunshine every detail is clearly visible as I sit with the shutters wide open and eat my breakfast. The foreground is a level plain of rice-fields, which stretches away for three or four miles to where the first gentle ascent is marked by a line of villages and trees, and in some

FUJI OVER THE RICE-FIELDS OF SUZUKAWA

THE FLOWERY MOORLAND

places, where irrigation is possible, the terraced fields climb a little way up the mountain. Above them is a band of cultivated country, the general effect of it dark green, varied by stripes of paler green fields. At first the forms are sharply defined, but higher up the whole becomes a blue-green mass. Next above this is a band of moorland with no trees on it, lighter and warmer in color, the grasses and plants which cover it tinged with yellow or orange by the autumn. As the morning sun shines on it little blue shadows, in spots and waving lines, mark the undulations of its surface. This belt of moorland reaches to the height of about five thousand feet, and is very rich in flowers. Above it, again, is a great band of forest; the warm color of the deciduous trees at its lower edge gradually merges into the dark blue-green of the pines, which mount a long way up on the summits of the ridges that at this point seam the surface of the mountain. It is over this forest-land that the morning clouds generally begin to form. As I write, a little one, that looks like a puff of white steam, is beginning to float over the trees, and this will grow until in an hour's time the upper part of Fuji will be invisible. The well-defined gullies are a light orange-red tint, and the contrast between them and the dark pines on the dividing ridges is the strongest opposition of color on Fuji, except that where the snow and the black lava meet at its summit. As the gullies ascend and the pines disappear the color again becomes more uniform, dark gray with a tinge of Indian red, the red disappearing and the gray becoming a rich purple as it runs up in irregular points and lines among the lower snows. Only the very highest band is a solid white; on the left of the truncated top is Kenga-mine, the highest point of the crater's edge, and next it a flat line shows where the Murayama path enters; to the right of this a well-marked ridge of lava runs high up into the snow, and can be traced down to the moorland, cutting off the Hōei-zan portion from the rest of the mountain. Beyond this ridge are two flatter curves—the summits of Jizotaké and Kwannon-také—on the eastern side of the crater. The general outline of the mountain on the left is one simple curve, the almost level line where it begins to ascend from the Fuji-kawa River becoming steeper and steeper towards the top. The most distinct acceleration of grade is where the forests end and the ridges of lava begin. The outline on the right is broken just above the pine-clad ridges by the projection of Hōeizan, and again at the top of the moorland by another smaller hill—Tsurugi-zan; and the effect on this side is not so much a curve as two inclined planes, the first from Kwannon-také to Hōeizan, the second from there to the moorland, after which it becomes an undulating line of mounds leading away to the Ashitaka range of older mountains. On this right side there is much less variety of color, a sharp ridge of warm orange lava makes a crest to Hōei-zan, but the great cup-like hollow behind it and the treeless slope below it are one uniform gray. Nearly two centuries have passed since the eruption which altered this outline of Fuji and destroyed the vegetation, and many more will have to elapse before the ashes are sufficiently disintegrated to entice back the trees and flowers.

AUTUMN IN JAPAN

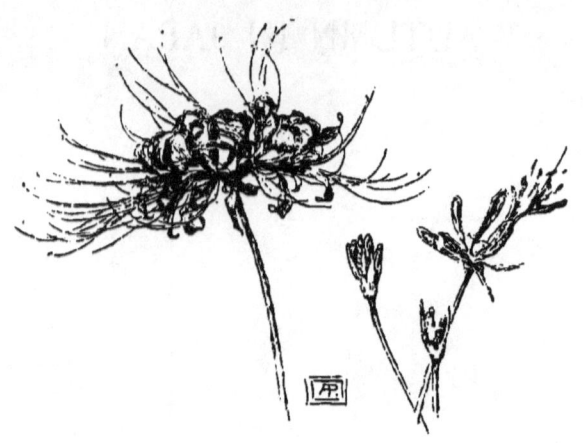

THE AUTUMN LILY

AUTUMN IN JAPAN

FROM the spring-time, when I reached Japan in the rain and began to grumble at the weather, and all through the damp and the downpour of the summer months, I had been consoled by the promises of my friends. They assured me that when the autumn came I should have week after week of glorious sunshine, a clear fresh air, and probably not a wet day between Michaelmas and Christmas. Either the season was an exceptional one, or else this is a cherished myth; there certainly were more fine days in October and November, but not a week passed without one or two days when work out-of-doors was impossible. They talked, too, of the glory of the maples, of hill-sides and rocky ravines clothed with scarlet and crimson, and their enthusiasm in this matter was am-

FIELDS NEAR HAMAMATSU

ply justified, but no one had told me of the beauty of the lilies of the field, which decorate so many of the banks between the rice patches with their tassels of glowing scarlet. I saw them first near Hamamatsu, a pleasant town on the Tokaido, which I reached on the 16th of September, after a little tour in the interior; their brilliant color at once attracted me, and I hastened to make drawings of them, for my passport had almost expired, and I feared that I might not find them elsewhere. There was no need to be in such a hurry, for they seem to grow abundantly wherever they get a chance. Hamamatsu was quite unlike any other Japanese town I had seen; the houses had a projecting upper story and broad overhanging roofs, and the principal trade seemed to be in toys. There were shops full of drums and kites, and dolls with all their belongings, and the thousand and one things which the Japanese delight in giving to their beloved children. As I passed a little garden I saw what looked like a fearful atrocity—dozens of babies' heads, pale and gray as if in death, cut off at the neck and impaled on short

THE EDGE OF THE TOKAIDO, NEAR HAMAMATSU

stakes, stood about the ground; but on coming nearer the mystery was explained: they were life-sized dolls' heads of papier-maché, put out to dry in the sun before receiving their final coat of paint. The neighboring villages were peculiar; every cottage was protected from the winds by a high hedge of clipped yew, and the street seemed to pass between two green walls, over which the heavily thatched roofs just peeped. The openings gave a glimpse of courtyards and cottage fronts where women and men were hard at work, threshing their beans of many colors and spreading them on mats to dry, weaving blue cotton cloths, or winding off the skeins of shining yellow silk. The typhoon a fortnight earlier had strewn the Tokaido with pine-trees; a passage wide enough for a jinrikisha to pass had been sawn through some of the great prostrate trunks, and others were still supported by their mangled limbs, so that we could squeeze under them. They sadly impeded the work of a company of white-clad engineers, who, with all the latest military contrivances, were laying a field-telegraph along the road. What a contrast were these sons of change to the fishermen returning from their morning's work with heavy loads of bonito, and to the peasants with their simple and primitive implements, all working and living as they have done for centuries past! Politics and changes of government matter very little to them; the rice crop and the take of fish are affairs of much more importance; they are the real life of a country, preserving its habits, costumes, and traditions, and staving off for a time the influences of railroads and steamships, which threaten to reduce man's condition throughout the world to one dull level of uniformity.

Fortunately they form a solid majority in every land, a mass not easily moved, and even in progressive Japan it will be a long time before ill-cut trousers and steam-ploughs replace the kimono and the spade. The Tokaido Railway takes you in twelve hours from Hamamatsu to Kōbe, and while waiting till a new passport came from Tōkyō I had time to see a little more of the beautiful country around that hospitable port. The shores near Suma and Maiko, a little to the westward, are picturesque, and close by is the Strait of Akashi, through which a constant stream of traffic passes, ships of all kinds and sizes, from the little fishing-boats towed from the beach, to the big steamers from Europe and America. The island of Awaji lies across the entrance to the Inland Sea, leaving a narrow passage at each end; but the tide rushes so violently through the Naruta Channel to

THE ISLAND OF AWAJI, FROM MAIKO

the south, between Awaji and Shikoku, that it is often unnavigable, and most of the shipping comes this way. There are the remains of a Daimio's castle at Akashi; the main building is gone, and the plateau on which it stood is now a garden with tea-booths, but the foundation walls, the corner turrets, and the moat show what an important stronghold it must have been; and the view from it, down the Inland Sea to the west, over to the Shikoku Mountains on the south, and eastward to Osaka Bay and the hills of Yamato, is extensive and very fine in its outlines. At Maiko

ON THE SHORE NEAR MAIKO, THE STRAIT OF AKASHI TO THE RIGHT

there is a grove of curiously blown and twisted pine-trees, with the quaint forms which are loved by all artists, especially by the Japanese; and near Suma, wherever the wiry grasses had got a foothold among the sand, the shore was gay with scarlet lilies. The botanic name of this flower, which is really more like an amaryllis than a lily, is *Nerine japonica*. Its Japanese name is not so easy to determine, for wherever I went it had a different one; some of these names are shiwata-bana, teku-sari, chiridji, and ushi-no-ninniku (cow-garlic), but I think the commonest is higam-bana (equinox flower), and the best, for its opening marks the change of the season, the beginning of the end. It is probably because of this that, beautiful as it appears to European eyes, to the Japanese it is a flower of ill omen, associated in their minds with death and decay, and never used in art or in floral arrangements. The children, indeed, gather great armfuls of it; but they never take it inside their homes; the great bunches they have collected are either scattered among the family tombstones or left to wither on the foot-paths. They seem to like picking it because its juicy stem snaps so easily, and often amuse themselves as they sit by the road-side by breaking the stalks half through, leaving them hanging in regular joints, much as our children make dandelion or daisy chains. Near a little graveyard set down among the rice-fields the flowers grew in great profusion, making a gorgeous splash of brilliant color as a foreground to the gray stones, the yellowing grain, and the pale blue distant hills. The rice was ripening fast, and flocks of

LILIES BY THE SHORE, SUMA

rice-birds flew hurriedly across as they were chased from field to field by shouting boys. I wish I had made a sketch of a Japanese scarecrow; there were plenty of them about, and I never saw one without laughing; they were full of quaint humor and invention, and the little birds seemed to enjoy them as much as I did. They recalled the remark of a stranger in a fly-haunted parlor in South Carolina, where a small clock-work windmill revolved in the centre of the table. I asked whether it drove the flies away, and the owner re-

A GRAVEYARD AT SUMA

plied, "At first it scared them some, but now they come in to ride round on it." The shore was always full of life and activity; bronzed fishermen, naked except for a narrow white loin-cloth, were launching their boats or hauling them ashore, towing along the beach, pulling up nets, or chanting as they rowed their heavy craft, standing up and pushing the long bent oars with a forward jerk, in the same way that a gondolier works. The smaller sailing-boats are all rigged with

HILLS BEHIND KŌBE

the simple oblong sail which is so often shown in Japanese drawings, made of narrow strips of cotton cloth loosely laced together; the larger ones have a jib and a jig-sail as well.

Futa-tabi, Maya-san, and the other hills which rise behind Kōbe are as well worth seeing as the shore, full of picturesque walks; the country at the back of them, commonly called " Aden " by the foreign residents, on account of its barenness, is a curious waste of disintegrating granite, seamed and furrowed by the heavy rains, where only some scrubby bushes find a precarious foothold on the shifting soil. Coolies from the neighboring villages come and cut these for firewood, and carry the heavy fagots for miles to earn a few halfpence. In Arima, one of the hill villages, there are hot ferruginous springs where hundreds of people go to bathe; but the arrangements are not so primitive as those I saw at Yumoto; the baths and dressing-rooms are private enough for the shy foreigner. There is so much iron in the water that you come out of it covered with a red deposit which takes some days of washing to remove. On this excursion, as my boots were in hospital, I tried Japanese foot-gear—thick cotton socks and straw sandals; they were very light and comfortable at first, but after a time I was conscious of every little pebble I trod on, and I got back to Kōbe with a good deal of pain and many blisters. Foreigners who have often worn them get hardened between the toes, and many good walkers and mountaineers use them habitually; heavy boots are an encumbrance when not on your feet, and though the straw sandals are quickly worn out, a few extra pairs are no serious addition to your baggage.

On the 6th of October I had finished my drawings among the pines and the sand hills, and a new passport had come, which gave me permission to wander for three months longer through the provinces near the Tokaido, so I bid farewell to my good friends and the comfortable club-house in Kōbe, and Matsuba once more left his wife and family to follow my fortunes.

Our destination was Maibara, a little town on Lake

A BAMBOO YARD AT MAIBARA

Biwa, not many miles from Hikone. As I passed it by rail I had noticed that the flooded fields on the margin of the lake were covered with a blue-flowered water-plant, a good foreground to the blue water and the distant mountains, and I hoped for blue skies to complete the picture, but they came only at rare intervals. On a piece of waste

BLUE WATER-WEED

ground near my tea-house a travelling theatre had been erected, a structure of bamboo poles with mats hung over them, which was not calculated to keep an audience dry, and not once during my stay were the company able to give a performance. The manager occupied the room next mine; he was an excellent performer on the samisen, and a pious man withal. Every morning from seven till half-past he said his prayers, repeating in a monotonous singsong voice a sentence which sounded to me like " Ya ya yura no," and tapping two blocks of wood together to keep time. He belonged to the Shingon sect of Buddhists.

THE TRAVELLING THEATRE, MAIBARA

The prayer formula of the Monto sect, one of the most popular and powerful, owning the great Hongwanji temples which are found in all large towns, is, "Namu Amida Butsu," while the followers of Nichiren, as they beat their drums, murmur constantly, "Namu myōhō renge kyō."

We soon became good friends, the manager and I, and he spent many hours in my room drinking tea, looking at my sketches, and in such conversation as my rudimentary knowledge of the language permitted, but unfortunately I never had an opportunity of seeing him act. When I left he presented me with a printed cotton towel in an ornamental wrapper, and I gave him a penny black-lead pencil, and we parted with mutual expressions of esteem. I had other visitors too: the station-master and the chief of police wanted to see my pictures, and Takaki, O Shige San, and little Kazu, with the brown velvet eyes, came over from Hikone to call on me, and arranged to meet me at the Nagahama matsuri. This annual festival takes place in the middle of October, and seems to be a gathering-ground for all the country-side. In many respects it was very like a country fair in England, but the main event on all the three days is the perambulation of large triumphal cars, called yama, on which companies of children give dramatic performances. I was fortunate in having a brilliantly fine day, and as I bowled along the five miles of level road from Maibara in a kuruma with two good runners, I passed troops of people in holiday attire, old peasants, gayly dressed young girls, and wandering friars with huge bamboo hats that looked like bushel baskets. The town was gayly decorated with flags and with lanterns bearing the device of the city, and crowds were pouring into it by road and rail and boat; for Nagahama is a busy port at the northern end of Lake Biwa, and a regular service of steamers runs between there and Otsu, at the southern end. This mixture of things ancient and modern in Japan always seems amusing, especially when, as in Nagahama, there is not much of the modern. The row-boats which came in with their loads of passengers were of unvarnished wood, decorated with black patterns on the bows, and, except the police and the railway officials, I saw very few men in European dress; there certainly were no women in anything but their own becoming costume, and I was the only foreigner in the town. My landlord had been thoughtful enough to engage a place for me in a tea-house opposite which the yama stopped and gave a performance: all the partitions had been removed, and the floor, divided into squares by low movable railings, was covered with family parties who had brought their own cushions and provisions.

My heart was filled with covetousness as I saw the fine old lacquer bento boxes which they produced after care-

LAUNCHING A BOAT

fully removing many silk wrappings. There are twelve yama in the town, each owned by a different guild or society, the members of which teach the children their parts, provide dresses for their play, and accompany the yama on the festival days. The cars are huge things, taller than most of the Japanese houses, and quite fill up the nar-

LAKE BIWA WITH FLOODED RICE-FIELDS, NEAR MAIBARA

row streets; they are built on solid wooden wheels, and are dragged about by strings of coolies, the young men of the guild dancing and shouting in front of them, waving fans by day and lanterns after dark to direct the coolies' movements, while the older members follow in white-curtained carts. The wood-work around the stage is lacquered, gold and black and red, with elaborate brass ornaments, and the pagoda-like roof which covers it is of burnished gold, surmounted with a dragon or phœnix or other mythical animal. The part behind the stage is enclosed with hangings, Chinese embroideries, Persian rugs, or silk brocades, and two of them had fine pieces of Flemish tapestry, which must have come over with the Dutch centuries ago; the buxom ladies and knights in armor looked odd, and yet pleasantly familiar, and my heart went out to the expatriated strangers, so lonely amid that Eastern crowd. In front of each stage hung a bunch of "gohei," the twisted strips of white paper which are the universal emblem of the Shinto religion, the only simple things among the masses of gorgeous color, and they seemed to give the key-note to the whole; for Shinto is, above everything else, an ancestor-worship, a religious respect for the country and for the men whose heroic deeds still inspire its people, and the short dramas which the children acted were all founded on old stories—how Yoritomo's son sacrificed his life to save the young Mikado, and other well-known motives from Japanese history. The boys were admirably trained and beautifully dressed; they rolled their eyes and grimaced in exactly the same way as their elders of the profession, and the crowd vigorously applauded their facial contortions. In one company there was a little mite of two years old; he had not to speak at all, only to cry out once or twice, but he knew his part as well as the rest, and always looked up at his boy father at the right moment. During the afternoon I walked round the town, first to the Buddhist temple, the great hall of which was crowded with people sleeping, eating, and praying, and then up the long avenue leading to the Shinto temple of Hachiman. It was lined with stalls and booths for refreshments of all kinds, with conjurers, purse-trick men, lucky wheels, quack-medicine venders, and so on, and near the big granite torii and lanterns were the market-gardeners with dwarf pines, oranges laden with fruit, camellias, and other trees. One had nothing but orchid-plants, none of them, unfortunately, in flower. I joined a large circle of spectators who were watching a scriever, which is, I believe, the professional name for the artists who draw on the flag-stones; this one had no pavement, so he prepared an even ground by sprinkling some light gray sand over the dusty road; his colors were bags of black, white, red, and blue sand; from one of these he took a handful, and drew his design by letting the powder run from his closed fist in a line which varied in thickness as he tightened or loosened his grasp. He wrote or drew in this way with wonderful rapidity as he squatted on the ground, and he talked all the time, obliterating each drawing as soon as he had finished it. I watched him draw a figure of a girl, and he began by putting down the spots of the pattern on her kimono with blue, then added the shadow lines of the dress, relieved it here and there with white, sketched the face and hands in red, and finally added a bold outline in black, which completed the picture, thus working in that reverse way to our natural instincts which you so often notice in this land of Topsy-turvydom.

As evening approached, all the yama began to collect in the square in front of another Shinto temple, where the great Hachiman car with colossal swords, and the Mikoshi, a shrine carried about on men's shoulders, were already placed. In the river on one side of this square many boats were moored, spread with rush mats and with the red blankets which have become so common in Japan, and in them people were picknicking; over the bridge which crossed it the unwieldy structures were dragged from the town by shouting crowds; each in turn gave a final performance in front of the temple, and was then drawn aside to make room for the next. This began at half-past five, and it was eleven o'clock before the last of

ONE OF THE "YAMA" AT THE NAGAHAMA MATSURI
From a printed programme sold on the street

them had been ranged with the others to the right of the temple steps. As night came on they were covered with big lanterns, the stages were lighted by lamps in glass shades, and attendants with candles on long sticks illuminated the face of each little actor while he was speaking. When the six gorgeous yama with their attendants and gayly dressed performers were all drawn up in line against

SOME HATS AT THE NAGAHAMA MATSURI

a background of solemn cryptomerias, with an excited crowd dancing and waving lanterns in front of them, the spectacle was more beautiful than any words of mine can suggest. In spite of the excitement, I saw only one quarrel; a young man, in order to get nearer to the stage, had pushed past a big coolie, who had evidently taken as much saké as he could carry, and for a few seconds I thought there would be a fight; but a bystander pointed out to the indignant man that the youth had to get nearer because he was short-sighted and wore spectacles, and peace was at once restored. On the way back to our tea-house, where my friends from Tennenji had dined with me, we passed a street full of stalls, with pipes and pouches, cheap jewelry, hair-pins and combs, and many other knick-knacks suitable for presents. I wanted a few of them, and found that O Shige San was a talented shopper; she had her limit, ten sen, and usually succeeded in getting the article for that sum, whatever the original price might have been. As I wandered round early the next morning I found that the yama had already been moved to their stations in various

THE TEMPLE GARDEN, SEIGWANJI

streets, and were being cleaned up in preparation for the day's performances. The town is studded with tall fireproof go-downs, in which the precious vehicles are safely stored during the rest of the year.

Near Maibara there were large orchards of persimmons with brilliant-colored fruit, which, as Andrew Marvel says of the oranges, "hang like gold lamps in a green night." They were particularly beautiful in the well-designed garden of Seigwanji, where I made some sketches. It is a fine example of a temple garden, and some massive evergreen oaks form an impressive background to the gray stones, the carefully trained pines, and the trimly clipped shrubs; but except for the persimmons, a few reddening maple leaves, some late blooms of platycodon, and the scarlet berries of a little ardisia, it was all green and gray.

In the cottage gardens near Suzukawa, a little station on the Tokaido to the south of Fuji where I made a short halt late in October, I began to see some chrysanthemum flowers; they were not particularly fine or effective, but I found plenty to paint there, and wished very much that the days and my remaining weeks in Japan were not getting so short. The village lies behind a range of sand dunes, which are overgrown with ancient pines, and beyond them is the shore of Suruga Bay, a grand expanse of gray volcanic sand, called by the Japanese

MINIATURE PAGODA IN THE TEMPLE GARDEN, SEIGWANJI

Tago-no-ura, where fishermen are always hauling at nets in lines of naked brown figures against the blue sea, or wandering back in groups across the sands in long dark-blue coats, with pale-blue and white handkerchiefs tied over their heads, carrying their nets and parcels of fish wrapped in straw. At my tea-house, the Koshuya, I reaped the result of their labors, and got excellent dinners of red or gray tai, lobsters, and huge prawns, cooked by a man who was a real artist and took a pride in his profession.

The first really fine chrysanthemums I saw were in Yokohama, when I got back there early in November; I was disappointed to find that they were in temporary sheds put up to protect them from rain and sun, and not in masses out-of-doors, as I expected to see them; but they were excellently grown, and in the softened light of the oil-paper shades their colors showed to great advantage. The plants are treated much as they are with us, raised in pots from cuttings taken in the spring, and encouraged with plenty of manure until the buds are formed; before flowering they are removed from their pots and planted out in bold groups of color in the beds which have been prepared for them. Some plants are reduced to a single stem, on which only one enormous blossom is allowed to develop; these are generally arranged in a line, with each flower stiffly tied to a horizontal bamboo support, and the effect is very sad; but the excellence of the gardeners is best shown in growing large bushes, which have been known to carry as many as four hundred flowers of medium size, all in perfect condition, on the same day. An English gardener who had visited every show within reach of Tōkyō, including the Emperor's celebrated collection in the palace grounds, told me that he had seen no individual blossoms equal to the best dozen or so at a first-rate London exhibition, but that these great plants with their hundreds of flowers were tri-

ALFRED PARSONS.

A CHRYSANTHEMUM SHOW AT YOKOHAMA

umphs of horticulture. The most curious examples of chrysanthemum-growing were to be seen in the Dangozaka quarter of Tōkyō. The long hilly street is bordered on each side with gardens enclosed with high bamboo fences, and in every one, by paying three rin, you could see groups of life-size figures mainly covered with chrysanthemum leaves and flowers. They represented scenes from history, the drama, or Buddhist mythology, and were constructed with frame-works of bamboo, inside which the flower-pots were concealed, the shoots being brought through the openings and trained over the outer surface. The heads and hands were made of painted wood, and swords and other accessories were added to make them more life-like; the draperies of living leaves and flowers were skilfully arranged in large folds, and, as in most of the popular shows, they depicted the costumes of Daimio and Samurai of the past. At each entrance I was given a sort of play-bill, a roughly printed broad-sheet with a wood-cut and a description of the different groups, serving as an advertisement of the gardener's establishment. One of the finest places for autumn colors is the large garden behind the arsenal in the Koishikawa quarter, laid out by a former Prince of Mito as a quiet retreat for his old age. It covers several acres, and is certainly very beautiful, with its lakes and islands, solemn groves and shrines; but it is silent and deserted; the people are only admitted by a special permission; and I liked better the maples which line the banks of the Taki-no-gawa near Oji, where crowds were quietly enjoying themselves, sipping tea and saké as they sat in front of the tea-houses and gazed down on the trees, or strolling along in picturesque groups under the crimson canopy of foliage. The little river glides along with barely a ripple, and it reflected all the glory of the leaves which stretched over it in sprays of scarlet and gold, reminding me of a Japanese poem, " I wish to cross the river, but fear to cut the brocade on its surface." Another poem, dating from the time when it was customary to present silk or cloth to the Shinto gods instead of the "gohei," which now serve as a symbol, shows the national admiration of the autumn leaves: "This time I bring no offering; the gods can take the damask of the maple-trees on Tamukeyama."

There are many other trees in the rich flora of Japan which are as gay as the maples, though no others which show as great a variety of color; the dark leaves of the tulip-tree turn to a rich cadmium yellow, and the icho (Salisburia) is covered with pale gold, while many of the shrubs, grasses, and herbaceous plants with bright and varied tints help to relieve the solemn everlasting green of the pines and cryptomerias which clothe the eternal hills.

And so in a blaze of glory the Japanese year ends; but long before these last leaves have fallen the camellias are once more in flower, and continue until the plum blossom comes in February, a connecting link in the chain of beauty and flowers which encircles this happy land. One of my last days in Tōkyō was spent in showing my drawings to the students of the Uyeno School of Art, where Professor Okakura, the president, who combines with a good knowledge of Western art a great reverence for that of his own country, is attempting with no small success to keep up the artistic tradition, and to revive those artistic industries which were falling into decay. He had invited artists of other schools, some of whom had studied in Paris and Rome, but I was most interested in the remarks and questions of the purely Japanese students, and in their eagerness to discover any motive, besides the reproduction of nature, in work so different from their own.

At the Asakusa matsuri they were already selling emblems suited for the new year — the rice-rake to scrape

THE ARSENAL GARDEN, KOISHIKAWA, TŌKYŌ

together dollars; the rice-bag, daikon, and red tai, suggestive of good fare; and the target with an arrow in the bull's-eye, meaning, "May you hit the mark!" arranged round a mask of the goddess of fortune; and with a stock of these to bring me good-luck, I sailed away on the 10th of December across the dreary and flowerless Pacific.

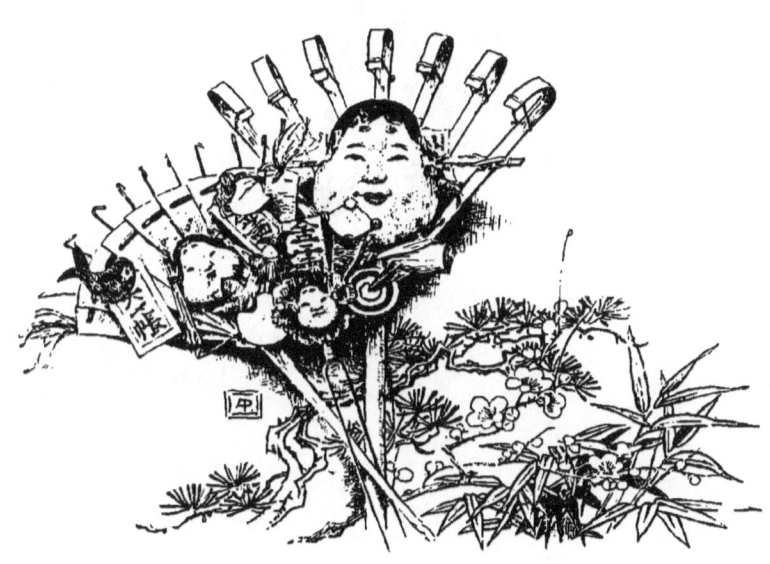

LYCHNIS GRANDIFLORA, MISAKA-TOGE

SOME WANDERINGS IN JAPAN

TRICYRTIS HIRTA, ATAMI

SOME WANDERINGS IN JAPAN

THE lakes which lie to the north of Fuji are not much visited by foreigners; they are rather difficult of access, and the accommodation in the tea-houses in that district is not luxurious; but for those who can walk well, and put up with ordinary Japanese food and lodging, the scenery will atone for everything. The old hills on the north once looked over a great sloping plain to the shore of Suruga Bay, but the upstart Fuji arose and blocked their view to the south; streams of lava poured from it, and rolled down till they were stopped by these buttresses of ancient rock, damming the rivers, and so forming this chain of lakes at their base. Where the lava has been covered with fine ashes, vegetation soon begins to conceal the work of destruction, but the larger flows resist all attempts at cultivation; they still stand in wide ridges above the rest of the country, gray lichens cover them, and dwarfed trees find a foothold in the crevices between their blocks. The winding tracks which lead across them are bad enough, for every little hump in the path is not a pebble which rolls aside as your foot touches it, but is a knob of solid rock, and it is your toe that has to give way; the untrodden part of the scrubby forest would stop any animal but an active monkey. We traversed one of the widest flows, called Aoki-ga-hara (green-tree moor), from the number of evergreens which grow over it, on the way between Shoji, the smallest, and Motosu, the largest of the lakes, walking for hours in single file along a narrow trail with hardly an opening anywhere in the dense foliage; it was late in the evening, and the imprecations in Japanese and English ought to have thrown a lurid light on that dusky path. The dividing-line between the lava and the older rock is as clearly visible now as it was on that day when the molten torrent was arrested in its course and piled itself in a solid wave against the immovable hills. Some subterranean settling must still be going on, for a few years ago the lakes began to rise, and they have remained at the higher level, so that as we rowed along the shore we could see below us the roofs of cottages and the fences of rice-fields, and forests of dead pines rose gaunt and bare out of the water. Of all the places I saw in Japan, Motosu seemed the most remote; the rise of the lake must have ruined many of the inhabitants, and a settled gloom seemed to hang over the few charcoal-burners, woodcutters, and fishermen who remain. We found rooms in an old tea-house, where fine wood-work, now blackened and decayed, showed signs of a former prosperity which will hardly revive unless prices rise, for when we left the next morning the landlord sadly presented us with a bill for nineteen sen (about sixpence), which for two foreigners and two servants came to a very modest sum per head. We crossed the lake by boat, and were landed at the foot of a trackless hill-side, overgrown with tall grasses and wild flowers, through which it was difficult to walk, but our local guides soon found a path which led us in the direction of the Fujikawa. Here we were off the volcanic soil, the beeches and other trees were magnificent, and in one wood we walked between banks of maidenhair fern (*Adiantum pedatum*) growing five or six feet high. How well I remember that day of glorious sunshine, the view back over the lake with Fuji towering

TAGO-NO-URA

behind it, the mountain road through forests with new trees and plants at every turn, the gaudy butterflies, the long zig-zag descent by the pine-clad spur which brought us to the Suzukawa Valley, and the gorgeous sunset as we whirled down the rapids to Shimoyama. There are five lakes in the chain, Motosu, Shoji, Nemba, Kawaguchi, and Yamanaka, and they descend in level from Motosu on the west to Yamanaka on the east. Nemba lies in a hollow of wooded hills, with a couple of partially drowned villages on its shore, in which the cottage roofs are strangely constructed, and the people wear long knickerbockers of blue striped cotton. Kawaguchi is the most beautiful of them all; its waters have only risen a foot or two, so that no damage has been done except the submersion of a few fields, and Funatsu and Kodachi, with picturesque old temples and cottages shaded with gourds, like Jonah's, are thriving towns compared with the other lake-side hamlets.

I was staying at Yoshida, within easy walking distance of Funatsu, in the early part of September, when all the countryside was keeping the Bon festival in memory of the dead—a sort of Japanese All-Souls day which lasts for a week. Fires were lighted at night on all the hill-sides; the path leading up to every little temple could be traced by a line of blazing spots, and the great lonely slope of Fuji was dotted with them here and there, marking the positions of the rest-houses and the few scattered huts of grass-cutters and charcoal-burners. I have seen the same thing in Switzerland, near Martigny, where on the eve of St. John's

COTTAGES AT NEMBA

day every cattle-tender far up the mountains greeted his distant neighbors with a bonfire. This part of the ceremony is called, in Japanese, *hi-matsuri* (fire festival). Other observances are placing offerings of food before the family graves, which in Yoshida were generally at the end of the back garden, and erecting a little altar in the house, on which dishes of rice, fruit, and sweetmeats are laid, and before which prayers are said.

We had a typhoon on the 4th of September, with such torrents of rain and gusts of wind that the houses had to be enclosed with their wooden shutters, and there was nothing to be done but lie on the floor in the darkness and listen to the turmoil of the elements outside. Suddenly, above all the other noises, I heard a monotonous chant, and, opening a crack in my shutters, I saw a procession of men, dressed only in "kasa" and straw rain-coats passing down the village street. Some of them carried big drums slung to poles, on which the others banged, while all of them groaned in unison a sentence which I could not catch. It was a long time before I could induce Matsuba to tell me what it all meant; but at last he confessed that it was done to drive away the storm-demon; he was evidently ashamed of this method of praying for fair weather, and explained that it was only in these out-of-the-way places his countrymen were so superstitious. Anyhow, it was efficacious, for the typhoon blew itself out during the night. There was more or less rain for some days after, but we had nothing again like that day's downpour, and I started in more promising weather for a walk over the hills to Kofu. From Funatsu I crossed a corner of Kawaguchi, and took a steep mountain road on the other side; some kind of matsuri was going on there too, and the lake was dotted with boatfuls of people beating drums and singing. The road we took is said in the guide-books to be practicable for jinrikishas, but the typhoon had completed the work of destruction which the heavy rains in July had begun, and there were very few yards of it left over which a wheeled vehicle could travel. On the other side of the pass, Misaka-toge, where I stayed to lunch and admire the view of Fuji, and to collect seeds of a grand red lychnis which grew there abundantly, we went through a village, Nakagawa, that had been almost destroyed by a torrent. The street and the gardens were filled with bowlders and gravel and fallen tree trunks, and the roofs only were visible above the mass of wreckage. The well-fitted timbers of a Japanese roof, especially when there is a heavy thatch over them, make it the least destructible part of the house; the lower part may collapse in a typhoon or earthquake, but the roof settles down over the ruins practically uninjured. I saw one near the Tokaido which had been taken off bodily by the wind and deposited in a field the other side of the road without losing its shape. I looked for the river which had done all this damage to Nakagawa, and found only a little, innocent, prattling brook about a yard wide.

Kofu is a busy place in the centre of a large silk-growing district. All the hill-sides around are covered with scrubby-looking mulberry bushes, and in the villages almost every cottage had its pile of golden cocoons, which the women were winding off into skeins as they sat and chattered by their doorways. As you pass Japanese houses in fine weather you see almost everything that is going on inside; they are set down close to the road, and the sliding-screens allow you to look right through to the garden at the back. When it is cold or wet all the wooden shutters are closed, and they have then a very sad and deserted appearance. I went to a very good theatre in Kofu, and afterwards to what might be called a wax-work show, but that the figures were

LAKE SUWA AND THE NAKASENDO MOUNTAINS, FROM KAMI-NO-SUWA

made of carved and painted wood, where the incidents of the murder of Ii-Kamonno-Kami were represented with a startling fidelity to nature. He was assassinated one winter's night in the streets of Tōkyō by the retainers of a rival Daimio, and the snowy ground showed to advantage all the details of disembowelled bodies and mangled limbs. The last two figures were mechanical. A retainer kneeling in front of the Daimio slowly opened a bloody handkerchief and showed him the head of his enemy, whereupon the Daimio's eyebrows went up and the corners of his mouth went down, giving him a most comical expression of horror.

The roads are wider here than in most parts of Japan, and there are comparatively few jinrikishas. Most of the travelling is done in basha, small wagonettes with no springs, which jolt the very life out of you. I engaged one to take me on to Lake Suwa, on the Nakasendo road, a journey of forty miles, and arrived there feeling like an aching jelly. After travelling a few miles from Kofu we came to a river where the bridge had been washed away. I and my baggage were ferried over, and the driver attempted to ford it, but the water was too deep for him, and I was left stranded with my impedimenta on a wide waste of pebbles. Fortunately the man with whom I had made my bargain had foreseen this possibility, and when I could get some coolies to help me with my baggage across half a mile of stones and bowlders, I found another basha waiting for me. All the first part of the journey was a long ascent through wooded, hilly country, with road-side villages at short intervals. In one of them, Tsutaki, where we stopped to change horses, a school treat was going on. The place was gayly decorated with lanterns and arches of leaves and paper flowers, and in the temple court-yard the children had made realistic figures, among them a life-sized tiger, ingeniously constructed with straws of different colors. The low wooden cottages, with broad eaves and stones piled on the top, looked very like Swiss chalets, except that they all had green roof crests, sometimes of iris, but more often of a bunchy kind of lycopodium which the natives called yuwashiba. Almost every one had a screen of bamboo on the south side, with gourds of different kinds growing up it and tumbling over the roof and the out-buildings. At last, with long spells of walking, very welcome as a rest from the weary jolting, we reached the tea-house at the top of the pass, and then rattled down a somewhat better road for about twelve miles, emerging at dusk into the broad mountain-guarded valley in which Suwa lies. The flat lands near the lake are intersected by little streams and canals, along which the peasants go to their work in long, narrow punts, very like those which are used for the same purpose in Picardy—another instance of the way in which similar conditions in widely distant countries lead to similer habits and inventions.

I stayed at Kami-no-suwa in a delightful tea-house, with clean polished wood-work, and quilts covered with a soft thin silk called kaiki, very pleasant and cooling to a mosquito-tortured skin. Cleanliness is the great luxury of the Japanese; their foot-gear is always removed before entering the house, so that the mats may not be soiled; the wood-work is never painted, stained, or varnished, but left with a well-planed surface, which shows its natural color; the ceilings are thin planks, slightly overlapping each other, the grain of each being carefully selected to combine with the lines in those next it; there are no hangings or fixed pieces of furniture to collect the dust, and no carpets to be taken up and shaken, so that spring cleaning, that terror of the Western house-keeper, is unnecessary; the whole room can be swept out every morning, the walls and ceiling rubbed with a duster, and there it is, all as neat as a

TOURISTS AT A WATERFALL

NIEGAWA, ON THE NAKASENDO

new pin. At Shimo-no-suwa, about three miles on, the Koshu-kaido, along which I had been travelling from Kofu, joins the Nakasendo, the central mountain road, one of the main routes between Kyoto and Tōkyō. A new road has been made most of the way, admirably engineered, with gentle gradients, but so badly executed that it had already fallen to pieces in some places, and it was covered with loose road-metal which made jinrikisha travelling very laborious. My men usually preferred the old steep road, which cuts off corners, and is solid though very rough, and after a couple of days I sent back all the jinrikishas except the one which carried my baggage, finding my own legs the best means of conveyance. From the Shiojiri Pass I looked back over Suwa, saw Fuji through the blue haze of a lovely autumn morning, a long way off, but still towering above all the other hills, and then dropped down into a new set of mountains, rivers, and valleys. The scenery of the Nakasendo gets more and more picturesque, until it reaches a climax in the valley of the Kisogawa, on which I first looked from the summit of the Torii Pass, four thousand and odd feet above the sea. Each village on the road had its own peculiarities of costume, architecture, and manufacture—cheap lacquer-ware, combs, pickles, and so on, and of all these Matsuba bought a stock, for it is the habit of every Japanese on his travels to take back with him "meibutsu," the characteristic productions of the places he has visited, as presents for those he has left at home.

There are many celebrated mountains in this district, each with its own special god and shrines, and I constantly met bands of pilgrims dressed in white, with long staves and big hats, or saw boat-loads of them going down

A LITTLE SHINTO SHRINE, NEAR THE NAKASENDO

the Kisogawa in the few places where it is navigable. After some days of glorious weather, with a sun which turned the wings of the myriad dragon-flies hovering over the rivers to spots of light, and made all clothing seem superfluous, I was suddenly arrested by a violent storm at a little village called Suwara. A number of pilgrims had been driven to shelter in the same tea-house; they spent the day in chanting prayers, ringing a little bell, and tapping blocks of wood together to mark the time; and they began it again at three o'clock the next morning, before starting on their trudge. The motive of these pilgrimages is not in the least penitential. Certain hardships have to be endured by every traveller in mountain regions, but the Japanese are good walkers and accustomed to simple living, and in their composition they have a large stock of intelligent curiosity which makes them enjoy all that is new and beautiful in the country through which they pass. The history and literature of their fatherland form a large part of their education, and almost every remarkable spot has some legendary or poetical association apart from its natural beauty; their religion teaches them, too, that not only temples and shrines are sacred, but that every poetic thought or heroic deed, every grand tree or rock or lovely landscape, has in it something of the divine.

On the banks of the Kisogawa, not far from Suwara, there is a large flat rock, which is called Nezame-no-toko, the Bed of Awakening, for here Urashima the fisher-boy, a sort of Japanese Rip Van Winkle, is supposed by some to have returned to real life after his long trance. The usual version of the story is this: Urashima lived with his parents at Yura, by the sea of Japan, helping them in their fishing; but one day his boat did not return, and he was given up for dead. He had met the Sea-god's daughter, who had taken him away to live with her and love her in an evergreen land. What seemed to him like a few weeks passed by in happiness, but at last he said, "My parents will be sorrowing for me; I must go back and comfort them," and he prevailed on his princess to spare him for a while. She gave him a casket, saying that as long as he kept it closed she would always be with him, but if he opened it, she and the evergreen land would be lost to him forever. He had really been away for centuries, his home had disappeared, and everything in Yura was changed. In despair he opened the forbidden box, a faint blue mist floated out from it across the sea, he turned from a handsome youth to an old decrepit man, and in a few minutes lay dead upon the shore, for in that box his princess had enclosed all the hours of their happy life.

No portion of the Nakasendo is finer than that near Midono; the valley narrows and the road in many places overhangs the rushing Kisogawa, the vegetation is luxuriant, walnuts, oaks, chestnuts, and maples shade the road, and great groves of bamboo wave their plumes in every little breeze which comes down from the mountains through the ravines in which they grow. By the river-side I noticed many fine-leaved plants; some old garden friends, and others new to me; yellow wagtails fluttered jauntily from rock to rock, and lines of swallows on the telegraph wires showed that autumn was at hand.

I turned off from the Nakasendo at Hashiba, where it begins to ascend the Magome Pass, and took a little cross-country track, turning eastward again up the valley of the Hirosegawa, which, after two days' walking, brought me to Iida and the banks of the Tenryugawa. This road was not mentioned in my guide-book, but Nakajima Sanju, the jinrikisha man who had accompanied me all the way from Kami-no-suwa, maintained that it was practicable, and that he could take my baggage through in his kuruma. He did

THE FERRY AT TOKIMATA

it, too, but I occasionally had to hire two extra men to help him, and in some places they and Matsuba had to carry kuruma, baggage and all. There was one long climb through a dense wood which particularly impressed me; I walked so far ahead of them that I could only just hear the continual cry, "Yo-sha! Yo-sha!" with which the men encouraged each other; the masses of foliage above me, the shrubs and ferns below them, enclosed me in a green maze; from under the arched roots of a colossal cryptomeria a clear little spring gushed out; occasionally a raucous-voiced jay flew across the path, or I had to stop and examine the huge toads, seven or eight inches long and almost as broad, that sprawled about on the road-side. When my men overtook me at a tea-house some miles farther on, one of them was carrying a brace of these toads skinned. They looked as big as the "poulet" of a cheap restaurant, and he told me that they were very good for weakly children.

At Tokimata I engaged a boat with five men to take me down the rapids as far as the Tokaido; the river was running high, and they would not do it for less than twenty-four yen—a good price for a journey of only ten or twelve hours; but when you remember that it takes them ten days or a fortnight to haul the boat back, it does not seem excessive. Don Pedro's remark, "What need the bridge much wider than the flood?" does not apply to most of the Japanese rivers; usually they are just a trickle of water among a wide bed of pebbles, which is filled after heavy rains with a raging torrent, but Lake Suwa serves as a reservoir for the Tenryugawa, and it always has enough water to be navigable. The boats used on it are about thirty feet long, flat-bottomed and flat-sided, with a square stern and a high, pointed bow; they are very loosely built and flexible, and the bottom boards are so thin that they wabble like a sheet of paper when passing over rough water or shallows. A heavy foot would break through them, and it is necessary to tread only on the bamboos which are laid lengthwise, resting on the cross-ribs.

ON THE TENRYUGAWA

My baggage was piled in the middle of the boat, and a seat arranged on it for Matsuba and myself; one man took the long stern oar while the other four worked in the bows, and within a few minutes of the start we were plunging down between high cliffs, charging at rocks which we only avoided by a few inches, swirling round in eddies at the foot of one rapid while the men got breath for the next, and until we stopped for our mid-day meal at the little vil-

THE VILLAGE STREET, ATAMI—VRIES ISLAND IN THE DISTANCE

lage of Nakabe there was no time to sketch, or think, or do anything but enjoy the wild, exciting race. The river twists, between high mountains, down a gorge with such sharp curves that it is often impossible to see any exit, and our boat would rush down, heading straight for a cliff against which the water dashed furiously; while one man in the bows whacked the side with his paddle for luck, and then stood ready with a pole, the other three pulled like mad, and just when I thought "we must come to grief this time," she would suddenly turn and swish round the corner into smoother water. The rapids continued to be amusing, though the fun was not quite so fast and furious, all the way to Kajima, where the mountains end and a broad plain begins; below here the river still ran swiftly, but smoothly, divided into several channels by long gravel banks, on which gray willows and bamboos grew, and snipe and herons congregated. We met strings of boats being laboriously towed along: the wind generally blows up stream, and they are

ON THE TENRYUGAWA, NEAR KAJIMA

able on these lower reaches to help themselves by hoisting a sail, but I shall never understand how they get their boats back through those upper rapids. It was getting dark when we passed through the ruins of the old Tokaido bridge, but in the dusk I could distinguish a row of familiar Noah's-ark-like forms; they were current-mills moored in the river; and then I knew what my day had lacked—the companionship of the man with whom I had passed so many hundreds of them on the Danube. There was nothing on the Danube quite so sporting as these rapids, but I think it would be possible to get through them in a decked canoe, such as those we used on that river. The pace is tremendous; we did the ninety miles from Tokimata to Naka-no-machi in ten hours of actual travelling, though the latter portion of the journey was on comparatively sluggish water.

About a month after this I stopped at Shizuoka, a large town on the Tokaido, where Ieyasu, greatest of the Shoguns, spent the end of his life in learned leisure, and where Keiki, the last of his successors, deposed in 1868, when the Mikado came to his own again, still lives quietly as a private gentleman. How much more dignified and reasonable is his Oriental acceptance of the accomplished fact than the restless scheming of some Western pretenders, who are unable to see that their ancestors, whether kings or emperors, owed their power to national feeling, and persist in a futile struggle against the inevitable! The Japanese obedience to law and authority, which must, however indirectly, be an expression of the will of the people, was never better shown than in the promptness with which the sword-bearing Samurai ceased to carry their weapons. The Samurai's blade had been for centuries his most sacred possession, a halo of poetry surrounded it, and the right to wear it in public distinguished him from the common herd; and yet when the imperial edict was issued in 1876 he laid it aside without a

AUTUMN-GRASS (SUZUKI)

murmur, and the curio-shops were soon full of swords, which a month before their owners would sooner have died than lose. It was no doubt very inconvenient to walk about always with two swords stuck in your obi, and perhaps he felt like the curate in the " Bab Ballads," who was forced by his mild rival to curl his hair and smoke—

> " I long have wished for some
> Excuse for this revulsion ;
> Now that excuse has come,
> I do it on compulsion ;"

but recent events show that though his ordinary life has become peaceful and bloodless, there has been no falling off in the pluck of a Japanese soldier.

Ieyasu was first buried at Kuno-zan, which I reached after about an hour's ride by jinrikisha from Shizuoka. The first part of the way was over a rice-covered plain, from which gay-colored hills, striped with white buckwheat, dark green tea, and pale green daikon, gradually rose, narrowing down towards the sea, and finally leaving only a strip of sandy soil, mostly planted with sugar-cane, between the steep cliffs and the shore. The little villages were odorous with drying fish, slices of bonito hanging in festoons in front of every cottage, and the shore was dotted with evaporating-tubs for getting salt. The mortuary temples, which served as a model for those afterwards built at Nikko, stand on the top of the cliff, and are reached by a zigzag flight of steps cut out of the rock; they are not so elaborate as the Nikko temples or the Shiba shrines, but have a severer beauty of their own, which nature has helped by decorating every stone and tree-trunk with silvery gray lichen, lovely in color against the background of red-lacquered buildings. The interior of the oratory, which, with its surrounding fence, has a roof of bronze, is mostly black and gold, and there the very affable priests who had shown me round held a little service in honor of Ieyasu, presenting me afterwards with the sweet wine and cakes which had been used as offerings. It is commonly said that the body of the great Shogun still lies under the simple stone monument behind the oratory, and that only a few hairs were removed and buried at Nikko; certainly this is the more impressive spot for a warrior's grave, with the wild hills behind, and the sea and coast spread out for miles below the towering cliff.

The road on to Okitsu, where I had to rejoin the railway, led me inland past Ryugeji, a temple where there are the finest specimens of the screw-palm (*Cycas revoluta*) to be seen in Japan, and then to the sea again at Shimizu, a nice little port, just opposite the sandy fir-clad spit of land called Mio-no-matsubara, enclosing a smaller bay in the great curve of Suruga, which often appears in Japanese pictures. This is the scene of a legend which has been dramatized, if you can call them dramas, for one of the classical No dances. It tells how a fisherman watching his nets saw a fairy alight on the sand and lay aside her robe of feathers; how he managed to steal the robe so that she could not fly away again, and only restored it to her when she consented to dance for him under the pine-trees one of the dances which are never seen by mortal eyes. Near the tea-house in Shimizu where I stopped to refresh there was a temple dedicated to Inari, the Shinto goddess of the rice-fields, whose shrines are guarded by foxes; the approach to it was under three avenues of small red wooden torii placed closely together, apparently votive offerings, for some of them were old and decayed and others quite bright and new.

At Numadzu, farther to the east on the Tokaido, but still on the shore of Suruga Bay, I again left the train and fol-

A RUSTIC BRIDGE AT DOGASHIMA, NEAR MIYA-NO-SHITA

lowed the course of the old road, from which the railway here diverges, as far as Mishima, and then, after crossing the ridge of mountain which forms the backbone of the Idzu Peninsula, descended to Atami on the western coast of Odawara Bay, a favorite watering-place during the winter months. The orange and banana trees testify to the mildness of its climate, and perhaps the geyser, which every fourth hour squirts out mud and boiling water by the village street, helps to keep up the temperature. Vries Island, with its eternally smoke-capped volcano, lies on the horizon away across the sea, and the natives believe that

AVENUES OF TORII IN FRONT OF AN INARI TEMPLE, NEAR SHIMIZU

there is a connection between the two, for whenever Vries is particularly active the geyser discharges more violently.

On the 3d of November I started with a friend from Yokohama to walk over the Ten Province Pass (Jikkoku-toge) to Hakone and Miya-no-shita. It was the Emperor's birthday, and all Atami was gay with flags; the national ensign with a red ball on a white ground fluttered everywhere. We mounted the steep street, and looked back at the village roofs and the deep blue water of Odawara Bay, and then turned into the woods of old camphor-trees surrounding the temple Ki-no-miya. Some of the camphors are enormous, and the largest of them are encircled with ropes of twisted straw and bunches of gohei, which show that they are sacred objects. Beyond the temple the path ascends, first through rice-fields and then up rough grassy hills, until it reaches the long plateau of turf where the Ten Province stone stands. Though so late in the year, there were still plenty of flowers. Down near Atami long sprays of hototogisu (*Tricyrtis*), with spotty purple flowers, hung out from the sandy banks, and by our path I saw Michaelmas daisies, golden-rod, dark-blue monk's-hood, sky-blue gentians, magenta-flowered garlic, thistles of various colors, wild chrysanthemums, pink or white with a gold centre, and the beautiful white stars of the grass of Parnassus. The sun was quite hot, and we pulled out some provisions and sat down on the grass near the stone to enjoy them and the marvellous view. To the north the snowy cone of Fuji rose high against the blue sky; between us and it the long crest of down-land was mostly covered with suzuki (*Eulalia japonica*), a lovely grass with tall plumes of seed which shine like silver gossamer, and the ranges of lower mountains were brilliant with the autumnal colors of maples and other trees; below us on the east lay the little peninsula of Manazura, jutting out into Sagami Bay, with a curve of rice-fields on each side of the narrow neck which connects it with the mainland, and beyond it the long straight line of the Pacific was broken only by Vries Island and its cloud of smoke; a succession of hilly promontories and little bays stretched all down the coast of Idzu to the southward, and returned northward again up the other side of the peninsula, past Joyama, with a lake-like inlet of sea, to Numadzu, where the great sweep of Suruga Bay began, bordered with sands and sunny rice-fields, and ended only at Kuno-zan, far to the westward. Our path went on along the downs,

JIZŌ SAMA, NEAR HAKONE

through suzuki, dwarf bamboo, and little stunted woods, until a deep descent led us down to the Hakone Lake, dark blue and sombre among its encircling hills; it then mounted once more for a short distance, passed the hot springs of Ashi-no-yu, and finally, while the grassy hills still glowed in the light of the setting sun, brought us down to the Fujiya at Miya-no-shita, where a delicious natural warm bath and a good dinner made a fitting termination to a glorious day.

At the bottom of a ravine almost perpendicularly below Miya-no-shita lies the little village of Dogashima, with a turbulent mountain stream and a very shaky bamboo bridge. The path and steps leading down to it are kept continually green by the overflow from the warm springs, and when I was there they swarmed with land-crabs, queer little beasts with bodies of dark green, blue, brown, or red, and a pair of light-colored claws, which they held up in a threatening attitude when I attempted to catch them. As they heard me approach they scurried off towards their holes, but they were so clumsy and so numerous that I could hardly help stepping on them.

One of the common objects by Japanese road-sides is the figure of Jizō, a Buddhist saint who is the helper of all who are in trouble, and especially the patron of travellers and children. Near the path between Hakone and Ashi-no-yu we passed a colossal presentment of him, carved in bold relief out of a mass of andesite rock, a very striking work of some ancient sculptor. It is said to have been done in a single night by that marvellously active saint Kobo Daishi, who, according to popular tradition, climbed all the mountains in Japan, and found time, when he was not preaching and confounding sceptics, to perform wonders in sculpture, painting, and calligraphy. Jizō, in the rudely carved statuettes by the way-sides, is a benevolent-looking priest, holding a traveller's staff in his right hand and a globe in his left. He stands on a lotus flower, and around his feet are piled many pebbles, placed there by wayfarers. The reason for the custom is this: On the banks of the So-dzu-kawa, the river of the lower world, there lives a hag who catches little children as they attempt to cross, steals their clothes, and makes them toil with her at her endless task of piling the stones on its shores. Jizō helps these children, and every pebble which is laid at his feet lightens the labor of some little one below. I never passed without adding my contribution, and if I cannot attribute my safety during my wanderings to his kindly aid, at least I am indebted to him for many a pleasant thought, and for the memory of many a lovely landscape or flower seen by his side.

BOOKS WITH ILLUSTRATIONS BY ALFRED PARSONS

A SELECTION FROM THE SONNETS OF WILLIAM WORDSWORTH. Illustrated by ALFRED PARSONS. 4to, Full Leather, Gilt Edges, $5 00. (*In a Box.*)

THE WARWICKSHIRE AVON. Notes by A. T. QUILLER-COUCH. Illustrations by ALFRED PARSONS. 8vo, Ornamental Half Leather, $2 00.

THE QUIET LIFE. Certain Verses by Various Hands: the Motive set forth in a Prologue and Epilogue by AUSTIN DOBSON; the whole Adorned with Numerous Drawings by EDWIN A. ABBEY and ALFRED PARSONS. 4to, Ornamental Leather, Gilt Edges, $7 50. (*In a Box.*)

OLD SONGS. With Drawings by EDWIN A. ABBEY and ALFRED PARSONS. With Mounted India Proof Frontispiece, left loose for framing. 4to, Ornamental Leather Cover, Gilt Edges, $7 50. (*In a Box.*)

PUBLISHED BY HARPER & BROTHERS, NEW YORK.

www.ingramcontent.com/pod-product-compliance
Lightning Source LLC
Chambersburg PA
CBHW022008220426
43663CB00007B/1011